Taoist Teachings

The Book of Lieh-Tzu (Lao Tzu, or Laozi) –
The History and Meaning of the Philosophy
and Beliefs of Taoism

By Lionel Tyler Giles

PANTIANOS
CLASSICS

Published by Pantianos Classics

ISBN-13: 978-1-78987-179-1

First published in 1912

Contents

TO

My Father

whose translation of Chuan Tzû

first awakened in me

the love of Taoist lore

Editorial Note

The object of the Editor of this series is a very definite one. He desires above all things that these books shall be the ambassadors of good-will between East and West. He hopes that they will contribute to a fuller knowledge of the great cultural heritage of the East, for only through real understanding will the West be able to appreciate the underlying Problems and aspirations of Asia to-day. He is confident that a deeper knowledge of the great ideals and lofty philosophy of Eastern thought will help to a revival of that true spirit of charity which neither despises nor fears the nations of another creed and colour.

J. L. CRANMER-BYNG

50 Albemarle Street
London, W. 1

Introduction

The history of Taoist philosophy may be conveniently divided into three stages: the primitive stage, the stage of development, and the stage of degeneration. The first of these stages is only known to us through the medium of a single semi-historical figure, the philosopher Lao Tzu, whose birth is traditionally assigned to the year 604 B.C. Some would place the beginnings of Taoism much earlier than this, and consequently regard Lao Tzu rather as an expounder than as the actual founder of the system; just as Confucianism--that is, a moral code based on filial piety and buttressed by altruism and righteousness--may be said to have flourished long before Confucius. The two cases, however, are somewhat dissimilar. The teachings of Lao Tzu, as preserved in the *Tao Tê Ching*, are not such as one can easily imagine being handed down from generation to generation among the people at large. The principle on which they are based is simple enough, but their application to everyday life is surrounded by difficulties. It is hazardous to assert that any great system of philosophy has sprung from the brain of one man; but the assertion is probably as true of Taoism as of any other body of speculation.

Condensed into a single phrase, the injunction of Lao Tzu to mankind is, 'Follow Nature.' This is a good practical equivalent for the Chinese expression, 'Get hold of Tao', although 'Tao' does not exactly correspond to the word Nature, as ordinarily used by us to denote the sum of phenomena in this ever-changing universe. It seems to me, however, that the conception of Tao must have been reached, originally, through this channel. Lao Tzu, interpreting the plain facts of Nature before his eyes, concludes that behind her manifold workings there exists an ultimate Reality which in its essence is unfathomable and unknowable, yet manifests itself in laws of unfailing regularity. To this Essential Principle, this Power underlying the sensible phenomena of Nature, he gives, tentatively and with hesitation, the name of Tao, 'the Way', though fully realizing the inadequacy of any name to express the idea of that which is beyond all power of comprehension.

A foreigner, imbued with Christian ideas, naturally feels inclined to substitute for Tao the term by which he is accustomed to denote the Supreme Being--God. But this is only admissible if he is prepared to use the term 'God' in a much broader sense than we find in either the Old or the New Testament. That which chiefly impresses the Taoist in the operations of Nature is their absolute impersonality. The inexorable law of cause and effect seems to him equally removed from active goodness or benevolence on the one hand, and from active, or malevolence on the other. This is a fact which will hardly be disputed by any intelligent observer. It is when he begins to draw inferences from it that the Taoist parts company from the average Christian. Believing, as he does, that the visible Universe is but a manifestation of the invisible Power behind It, he feels justified in arguing from the known to the unknown, and concluding that, whatever Tao may be in itself (which is unknowable), it is certainly not what we understand by a personal God--not a God endowed with the specific attributes of humanity, not even (and here we find a remarkable anticipation of Hegel) a *conscious* God. In other words, Tao transcends the illusory and unreal distinctions on which all human systems of morality depend, for in it all virtues and vices coalesce into One.

The Christian takes a different view altogether. He prefers to ignore the facts which Nature shows him, or else he reads them in an arbitrary and one-sided manner. His God, if no longer anthropomorphic, is undeniably anthropopathic. He is a personal Deity, now loving and merciful, now irascible and jealous, a Deity who is open to prayer and entreaty. With qualities such as these, it is difficult to see how he can be regarded as anything but a glorified Man. Which of these two views--the Taoist or the Christian--it is best for mankind to hold, may be a matter of dispute. There can be no doubt which is the more logical.

The weakness of Taoism lies in its application to the conduct of life. Lao Tzu was not content to be a metaphysician merely, he aspired to be a practical reformer as well. It was man's business, he thought, to model himself as closely as possible on the great Exemplar, Tao. It follows as a matter of course that his precepts are mostly of a negative order, and we are led straight to the doctrine of Passivity or Inaction, which was bound to be fatally misunderstood and perverted. Lao Tzu's teaching has reached us, if not in its original form, yet in much of its native purity, in the *Tao Tê Ching*. One of the most potent arguments for the high antiquity of this marvellous little treatise is that it shows no decided trace of the corruption which is discernible in the second of our periods, represented for us by the writings of Lieh Tzu and Chuang Tzu. I have called it the period of development because of the extraordinary quickening and blossoming of the buds of Lao Tzu's thought in the supple and imaginative minds of these two philosophers. The canker, alas! is already at the heart of the flower; but so rich and luxuriant is the feast of colour before us that we hardly notice it as yet.

Very little is known of our author beyond what he tells us himself. His full name was Lieh Yü-k'ou, and it appears that he was living in the Chêng State not long before the year 398 B.C., when the Prime Minister Tzu Yang was killed in a revolution. He figures prominently in the pages of Chuang Tzu, from whom we learn that he could 'ride upon the wind'.[1] On the insufficient ground that he is not mentioned by the historian Ssu-ma Ch'ien, a certain critic of the Sung dynasty was led to declare that Lieh Tzu was only a fictitious personage invented by Chuang Tzu, and that the treatise which passes under his name was a forgery of later times. This theory is rejected by the compilers of the great Catalogue of Ch'ien

Lung's Library, who represent the cream of Chinese scholarship in the eighteenth century.

Although Lieh Tzu's work has evidently passed through the hands of many editors and gathered numerous accretions, there remains a considerable nucleus which in all probability was committed to writing by Lieh Tzu's immediate disciples, and is therefore older than the genuine parts of Chuang Tzu. There are some obvious analogies between the two authors, and indeed a certain amount of matter common to both; but on the whole Lieh Tzu's book bears an unmistakable impress of its own. The geniality of its tone contrasts with the somewhat hard brilliancy of Chuang Tzu, and a certain kindly sympathy with the aged, the poor and the humble of this life, not excluding the brute creation, makes itself felt throughout. The opposition between Taoism and Confucianism is not so sharp as we find it in Chuang Tzu, and Confucius himself is treated with much greater respect. This alone is strong evidence in favour of the priority of Lieh Tzu, for there is no doubt that the breach between the two systems widened as time went on. Lieh Tzu's work is about half as long as Chuang Tzu's, and is now divided into eight books. The seventh of these deals exclusively with the doctrine of the egoistic philosopher Yang Chu, and has therefore been omitted altogether from the present selection.

Nearly all the Taoist writers are fond of parables and allegorical tales, but in none of them is this branch of literature brought to such perfection as in Lieh Tzu, who surpasses Chuang Tzu himself as a master of anecdote. His stories are almost invariably pithy and pointed. Many of them evince not only a keen sense of dramatic effect, but real insight into human nature. Others may appear fantastic and somewhat wildly imaginative. The story of the man who issued out of solid rock (p. 47) is a typical one of this class. It ends, however, with a streak of ironical humour which may lead us to doubt whether Lieh Tzu himself really believed in the possibility of transcending natural laws. His soberer judgment appears in other passages, like the following: 'That which has life must by the law of its being come to an end; and the end can no more be avoided than the living creature can help having been born. So that he who hopes to perpetuate his life or to shut out death is deceived in his calculations.' That leaves little doubt as to the light in which Lieh Tzu would have regarded the later Taoist speculations on the elixir of life. Perhaps the best solution of the problem is the theory I have already mentioned: that the 'Lieh Tzu' which we possess now, while containing a solid and authentic core of the Master's own teaching, has been overlaid with much of the decadent Taoism of the age that followed.

Of this third period little need be said here. It is represented in literature by the lengthy treatise of Huai-nan Tzu, the spurious episodes in Lieh Tzu and Chuang Tzu, and a host of minor writers, some of whom tried to pass off their works as the genuine relics of ancient sages. Chang Chan, an officer of the Banqueting Court under the Eastern Chin dynasty (fourth century A.D.), is the author of the best commentary on Lieh Tzu; extracts from it, placed between inverted commas, will be found in the following pages. In the time of Chang Chan, although Taoism as a philosophical system had long run its course, its development into a national religion was only just beginning, and its subsequent influence on literature and art is hardly to be over-estimated. It supplied the elements of mystery, romance and colour which were needed as a set-off against the uncompromising stiffness of the Confucian ideal. For reviving and incorporating in itself the floating mass of folklore and mythology which had come down from the earliest ages, as well as for the many exquisite creations of its own fancy, it deserves the lasting gratitude of the Chinese people.

[1] He is thus depicted in the design on the cover of this volume, taken from an illustrated work on Ink-tablets.

Book I - Cosmogony

Our Master Lieh Tzu dwelt on a vegetable plot in the Chêng State for forty years, and no man knew him for what he was. The Prince, his Ministers, and all the State officials looked upon him as one of the common herd. A time of dearth fell upon the State, and he was preparing to migrate to Wei, when his disciples said to him: 'Now that our Master is going away without any prospect of return-ing, we have ventured to approach you, hoping for instruction. Are there no words from the lips of Hu-Ch'iu Tzu-lin that you can im-part to us? Lieh Tzu smiled and said: 'Do you suppose that Hu Tzu dealt in words? However, I will try to repeat to you what my Master said on one occasion to Po-hun Mou-jên.

A fellow-disciple. Out of modesty, Lieh Tzu does not say that the teaching was imparted directly to himself.

I was standing by and heard his words, which ran as, follows:--

"There is a Creative Principle which is itself uncreated; there is a Principle of Change which is itself unchanging. The Uncreated is able to create life; the Unchanging is able to effect change. That which is produced cannot but continue producing; that which is evolved cannot but continue evolving. Hence there is constant pro-duction and constant evolution. The law of constant production and of constant evolution at no time ceases to operate.

The commentator says: 'That which is once involved in the desti-ny of living things can never be annihilated.'

So is it with the Yin and the Yang, so is it with the Four Seasons.

The Yin and the Yang are the Positive and Negative Principles of Nature, alternately predominating in day and night.

The Uncreated we may surmise to be Alone in itself.

'The Supreme, the Non-Engendered--how can its reality be proved? We can only suppose that it is mysteriously One, without beginning and without end.'

The Unchanging goes to and fro, and its range is illimitable. We may surmise that it stands Alone, and that its Ways are inexhaustible."

'In the Book of the Yellow Emperor it is written: "The Spirit of the Valley dies not; it may be called the Mysterious Feminine. The issuing-point of the Mysterious Feminine must be regarded as the Root of the Universe. Subsisting to all eternity, it uses its force without effort."

The Book of the Yellow Emperor is no longer extant, but the above passage is now incorporated in the *Tao Tê Ching*, and attributed to Lao Tzu.

'That, then, which engenders all things is itself unengendered; that by which all things are evolved is itself untouched by evolution. Self-engendered and self-evolved, it has in itself the elements of substance, appearance, wisdom, strength, dispersion and cessation. Yet it would be a mistake to call it by any one of these names.

*   *   *

The Master Lieh Tzu said: 'The inspired men of old regarded the Yin and the Yang as controlling the sum total of Heaven and Earth. But that which has substance is engendered from that which is devoid of substance; out of what then were Heaven and Earth engendered?

'They were engendered out of nothing, and came into existence of themselves.'

'Hence we say, there is a great Principle of Change, a great Origin, a great Beginning, a great Primordial Simplicity. In the great Change substance is not yet main est. In the great Origin lies the beginning of substance. In the great Beginning, lies the beginning of material form.

'After the separation of the Yin and the Yang, when classes of objects assume their forms.'

In the great Simplicity lies the beginning of essential qualities. When substance, form and essential qualities are still indistinguishably blended together it is called Chaos. Chaos means that all things are chaotically intermixed and not yet separated from one another. The purer and lighter elements, tending upwards, made the Heavens; the grosser and heavier elements, tending downwards, made the Earth. Substance, harmoniously proportioned, became Man; and, Heaven and Earth containing thus a spiritual element, all things were evolved and produced.'

*   *   *

The Master Lieh Tzu said: 'The virtue of Heaven and Earth, the powers of the Sage, and the uses of the myriad things in Creation, are not perfect in every direction. It is Heaven's function to produce life and to spread a canopy over it. It is Earth's function to form material bodies and to support them. It is the Sage's function to teach others and to influence them for good. It is the function of created things to conform to their proper nature. That being so, there are things in which Earth may excel, though they lie outside the scope of Heaven; matters in which the Sage has no concern, though they afford free play to others. For it is clear that that which imparts and broods over life cannot form and support material bodies; that which forms and supports material bodies cannot teach and influence for good; one who teaches and influences for good cannot run counter to natural instincts; that which is fixed in suitable environment does not travel outside its own sphere. Therefore the Way of Heaven and Earth will be either of the Yin or of the Yang; the teaching of the Sage will be either of altruism or of righteousness; the quality of created objects will be either soft or hard. All these conform to their proper nature and cannot depart from the province assigned to them.'

*   *   *

On one hand, there is life, and on the other, there is that which produces life; there is form, and there is that which imparts form; there is sound, and there is that which causes sound; there is col-

13

our, and there is that which causes colour; there is taste, and there is that which causes taste.

Things that have been endowed with life die; but that which produces life itself never comes to an end. The origin of form is matter; but that which imparts form has no material existence. The genesis of sound lies in the sense of hearing; but that which causes sound is never audible to the ear. The source of colour is vision; but that which produces colour never manifests itself to the eye. The origin of taste lies in the palate; but that which causes taste is never perceived by that sense. All these phenomena are functions of the principle of Inaction.

Wu Wei, Inaction, here stands for the inert, unchanging Tao.

To be at will either bright or obscure, soft or hard, short or long, round or square, alive or dead, hot or cold, buoyant or sinking, treble or bass, present or absent, black or white, sweet or bitter, fetid or fragrant--this it is to be devoid of knowledge, yet all-knowing, destitute of power, yet all-powerful.

Such is Tao.

*   *   *

On his journey to Wei, the Master Lieh Tzu took a meal by the roadside. His followers espied an old skull, and pulled aside the undergrowth to show it to him. Turning to his disciple Po Fêng, the Master said: 'That skull and I both know that there is no such thing as absolute life or death.

'If we regard ourselves as passing along the road of evolution, then I am alive and he is dead. But looked at from the standpoint of the Absolute, since there is no such principle as life in itself, it follows that there can be no such thing as death.'

This knowledge is better than all your methods of prolonging life, a more potent source of happiness than any other.'

*   *   *

In the Book of the Yellow Emperor it is written: 'When form becomes active it produces not form but shadow; when sound becomes active it produces not sound but echo.'

See note to introduction. This passage does not occur in the *Tao Tê Ching*.

When Not-Being becomes active, it does not produce Not-Being but Being. Form is something that must come to an end. Heaven and Earth, then, have an end, even as we all have an end. But whether the end is complete we do not know.

'When there is conglomeration, form comes into being; when there is dispersion, it comes to an end. That is what we mortals mean by beginning and end. But although for us, in a state of conglomeration, this condensation into form constitutes a beginning, and its dispersion an end, from the standpoint of dispersion, it is void and calm that constitute the beginning, and condensation into form the end. Hence there is perpetual alternation in what constitutes be timing and end, and the underlying Truth is that there is neither any beginning nor any end at all.'

The course of evolution ends where it started, without a beginning; it finishes up where it began, in Not-Being.

A paradoxical way of stating that there is no beginning and no end.

That which has life returns again into the Lifeless; that which has form returns again into the formless. This, that I call the Lifeless, is not the original Lifelessness. This, that I call the formless, is not the original Formlessness.

'That, which is here termed the Lifeless has formerly possessed life, and subsequently passed into the extinction of death, whereas the original Lifelessness from the beginning knows neither life nor extinction.' We have here again the distinction between the unchanging life-giving Principle (Tao), which is itself without life, and the living things themselves, which are in a perpetual flux between life and death.

That which has life must by the law of its being come to an end; and the end can no more be avoided than the living creature can help having been born. So that he who hopes to perpetuate his life or to shut out death is deceived as to his destiny.

The spiritual element in man is allotted to him by Heaven, his corporeal frame by Earth. The part that belongs to Heaven 'is ethereal and dispersive, the part that belongs to Earth is dense and tending to conglomeration. When the spirit parts from the body, each of these elements resumes its true nature. That is why disembodied spirits are called *kuei*, which means 'returning', that is, returning to their true dwelling-place.

'The region of the Great Void.'

The Yellow Emperor said: 'If my spirit returns through the gates whence it came, and my bones go back to the source from which they sprang, where does the Ego continue to exist?'

*   *   *

Between his birth and his latter end, man passes through four chief stages-infancy, adolescence, old age and death. In infancy, the vital force is concentrated, the will is undivided, and the general harmony of the system is perfect. External objects produce no injurious impression, and to the moral nature nothing can be added. In adolescence, the animal passions are wildly exuberant, the heart is filled with rising desires and preoccupations. The man is open to attack by the objects of sense, and thus his moral nature becomes enfeebled. In old age, his desires and preoccupations have lost their keenness, and the bodily frame seeks for repose. External objects no longer hold the first place in his regard. In this state, though not attaining to the perfection of infancy, he is already different from what he was in adolescence. In death, he comes to his rest, and returns to the Absolute.

*   *   *

Confucius was travelling once over Mount T'ai when he caught sight of an aged man roaming in the wilds. He was clothed in a deerskin, girded with a rope, and was singing as he played on a lute. 'My friend,' said Confucius, 'what is it that makes you so happy?' The old man replied: 'I have a great deal to make me happy. God created all things, and of all His creations man is the noblest. It has fallen to my lot to be a man: that is my first ground for happiness. Then, there is a distinction between male and female, the former being rated more highly than the latter. Therefore it is better to be a male; and since I am one, I have a second ground for happiness. Furthermore, some are born who never behold the sun or the moon, and who never emerge from their swaddling-clothes. But I have already walked the earth for the space of ninety years. That is my third ground for happiness. Poverty is the normal lot of the scholar, death the appointed end for all human beings. Abiding in the normal state, and reaching at last the appointed end, what is there that should make me unhappy? ;What an excellent thing it is,' cried Confucius, 'to be able to find a source of consolation in one-self!'

*   *   *

Tzu Kung was tired of study, and confided his feelings to Confucius, saying: 'I yearn for rest.' Confucius replied: 'In life there is no rest.'

'To toil in anxious planning for the future, to slave in bolstering up the bodily frame--these are the businesses of life.'

'Is rest, then, nowhere to be found? 'Oh yes!' replied Confucius; 'look at all the graves in the wilds, all the vaults, all the tombs, all the funeral urns, and you may know where rest is to be found.' 'Great, indeed, is Death!' exclaimed Tzu Kung. 'It gives rest to the noble hearted, and causes the base to cower.' 'You are right,' said Confucius. 'Men feel the joy of life, but do not realize its bitterness. They feel the weariness of old age, but not its peacefulness. They think of the evils of death, but not of the repose which it confers.'

*   *   *

Yen Tzu said: 'How excellent was the ancients' view of death!-- bringing rest to the good and subjection to the wicked. Death is the boundary-line of Virtue.

That is, Death abolishes all artificial and temporary distinctions between good and evil, which only hold good in this world of relativity.

'The ancients spoke of the dead as *kuei-jên* (men who have re-turned). But if the dead are men who have returned, the living are men on a journey. Those who are on a journey and think not of re-turning have cut themselves off from their home. Should any one man cut himself off from his home, he would incur universal repro-bation. But all mankind being homeless, there is none to see the er-ror. Imagine one who leaves his native village, separates himself from all his kith and kin, dissipates his patrimony and wanders away to the four corners of the earth, never to return:--what man-ner of man is this? The world will surely set him down as a profli-gate and a vagabond. On the other hand, imagine one who clings to respectability and the things of this life, holds cleverness and ca-pacity in high esteem, builds himself up a reputation, and plays the braggart amongst his fellow men without knowing where to stop:--what manner of man, once more, is this? The world will surely look upon him as a gentleman of great wisdom and counsel. Both of these men have lost their way, yet the world will consort with the one, and not with the other. Only the Sage knows with whom to consort and from whom to hold aloof.'

'He consorts with those who regard life and death merely as wak-ing and sleeping, and holds aloof from those who are steeped in forgetfulness of their return.'

*   *   *

Yü Hsiung said: 'Evolution is never-ending. But who can perceive the secret processes of Heaven and Earth? Thus, things that are di-minished here are augmented there; things that are made whole in one place suffer loss in another. Diminution and augmentation, fullness and decay are the constant accompaniments of life and death. They alternate in continuous succession, and we are not conscious of any interval. The whole body of spiritual substance progresses without a pause; the whole body of material substance suffers decay without intermission. But we do not perceive the process of completion, nor do we perceive the process of decay. Map, likewise, from birth to old age becomes something different every day in face and form, in wisdom and in conduct. His skin, his nails and his hair are continually growing and continually perishing. In infancy and childhood there is no stopping nor respite from change. Though imperceptible while it is going on, it may be verified afterwards if we wait.'

*　　*　　*

There was once a man in the Ch'i State who was so afraid the universe would collapse and fall to pieces, leaving his body without a lodgment, that he could neither sleep nor eat. Another man, pitying his distress, went to enlighten him. 'Heaven,' he said, 'is nothing more than an accumulation of ether, and there is no place where ether is not. Processes of contraction and expansion, inspiration and expiration are continually taking place up in the heavens. Why then should you be afraid of a collapse?' The man said: 'It is true that Heaven is an accumulation of ether; but the sun, the moon, and the stars--will they not fall down upon us? His informant replied: 'Sun, moon and stars are likewise only bright lights Within this mass of ether. Even supposing they were to fall, they could not possibly harm us by their impact.' 'But what if the earth should fall to pieces? 'The earth,' replied the other, 'is merely an agglomeration of matter, which fills and blocks up the four comers of space. There is no part of it where matter is not. All day long there is constant treading and tramping on the surface of the earth. Why then should you be afraid of its falling to pieces? Thereupon the man was relieved of his fears and rejoiced exceedingly. And his instructor was also joyful and easy in mind. But Ch'ang Lu Tzu laughed at them both, saying: 'Rainbows, clouds and mist, wind and rain, the four seasons--these are perfected forms of accumulated ether, and go to make up the heavens. Mountains and cliffs, rivers and seas, metals and rocks, fire and timber--these are perfected forms of agglomerated matter, and constitute the earth. Knowing these facts, who can say that they will never be destroyed? Heaven and earth form only a small speck in the midst of the Void, but they are the greatest things in the sum of Being. This much is certain: even as their nature is hard to fathom, hard to understand, so they will be slow to pass away, slow to come to an end. He who fears lest they should suddenly fall to pieces is assuredly very far from the truth. He, on the other hand, who says that they will never be destroyed has also not reached the right solution. Heaven and earth must of necessity pass away, but neither will revert to destruction apart from the other.

The speaker means that though there is no immediate danger of a collapse, it is certain that our universe must obey the natural law of disintegration, and at some distant date disappear altogether. But the process of decay will be so gradual as to be imperceptible.

Who, having to face the day of disruption, would not be alarmed?

The Master Lieh Tzu heard of the discussion, and smiling said: 'He who maintains that Heaven and earth are destructible, and he who upholds the contrary, are both equally at fault. Whether they are destructible or not is something we can never know, though in both cases it will be the same for all alike. The living and the dead, the going and the coming, know nothing of each other's state. Whether destruction awaits the world or no, why should I trouble my head about it?

*   *   *

Mr Kuo of the Ch'i State was very rich, while Mr Hsiang of the Sung State was very poor. The latter travelled from Sung to Ch'i and asked the other for the secret of his prosperity. Mr Kuo told him. 'It is because I am a good thief,' he said. 'The first year I began to be a thief, I had just enough. The second year, I had ample. The third year, I reaped a great harvest. And, in course of time, I found myself the owner of whole villages and districts.' Mr Hsiang was overjoyed; he understood the word 'thief' in its literal sense, but he did not understand the true way of becoming a thief. Accordingly, he climbed over walls and broke into houses, grabbing everything he could see or lay hands upon. But before very long his thefts brought him into trouble, and he was stripped even of what he had previously possessed. Thinking that Mr Kuo had basely deceived him,

Hsiang went to him with a bitter complaint. 'Tell me,' said Mr Kuo, 'how did you set about being a thief?' On learning from Mr Hsiang what had happened, he cried out: 'Alas and alack! You have been brought to this pass because you went the wrong way to work. Now let me put you on the right track. We all know that Heaven has its seasons, and that earth has its riches. Well, the things that I steal are the riches of Heaven and earth, each in their season--the fertilizing rain-water from the clouds, and the natural products of mountain and meadow-land. Thus I grow my grain and ripen my crops, build my walls and construct my tenements. From the dry land I steal winged and four-footed game, from the rivers I steal fish and turtles. There is nothing that I do not steal. For corn and grain, clay and wood, birds and beasts, fishes and turtles are all products of Nature. How can I claim them as mine?

It will be observed that Lieh Tzu anticipates here, in a somewhat different sense, Proudhon's famous paradox: 'La propriété c'est le vol.'

'Yet, stealing in this way from Nature, I bring on myself no retribution. But gold, jade, and precious stones, stores of grain, silk stuffs, and other kinds of property, are things accumulated by men, not bestowed upon us by Nature. So who can complain if he gets into trouble by stealing them?

Mr Hsiang, in a state of great perplexity, and fearing to be led astray a second time by Mr Kuo, went off to consult Tung Kuo, a man of learning. Tung Kuo said to him: 'Are you not already a thief in respect of your own body? You are stealing the harmony of the Yin and the Yang in order to keep alive and to maintain your bodily form. How much more, then, are you a thief with regard to external possessions! Assuredly, Heaven and earth cannot be dissociated from the myriad objects of Nature. To claim any one of these as your own betokens confusion of thought. Mr Kuo's thefts are carried out in a spirit of justice, and therefore bring no retribution. But your thefts were carried out in a spirit of self-seeking and therefore landed you in trouble. Those who take possession of property, whether public or private, are thieves.

By 'taking possession of public property', as we have seen, Lieh Tzu means utilizing the products of Nature open to all--rain and the like.

Those who abstain from taking property, public or private, are also thieves.

'For no one can help possessing a body, and no one can help acquiring some property or other which cannot be got rid of with the best will in the world. Such thefts are unconscious thefts.'

The great principle of Heaven and earth is to treat public property as such and private property as such. Knowing this principle, which of us is a thief, and at the same time which of us is not a thief?'

The object of this anecdote is to impress us with the unreality of mundane distinctions. Lieh Tzu is not much interested in the social aspect of the question. He is not an advocate of communism, nor does he rebel against the common-sense view that theft is a crime which must be punished. With him, everything is intended to lead up to the metaphysical standpoint.

Book II - The Yellow Emperor

The Yellow Emperor sat for fifteen years on the throne, and rejoiced that the Empire looked up to him as its head. He was careful of his physical well-being, sought pleasures for his ears and eyes, and gratified his senses of smell and taste. Nevertheless, he grew melancholy in spirit, his complexion became sallow, and his sensations became dull and confused. Then, for a further period of fifteen years, he grieved that the Empire was in disorder; he summoned up all his intelligence, exhausted his resources of wisdom and strength in trying to rule the people. But, in spite of all, his face remained haggard and pale, and his sensations dull and confused.

'The practice of enlightened virtue will not succeed in establishing good government, but only disorganize the spiritual faculties!

Then the Yellow Emperor sighed heavily and said: 'My fault is want of moderation. The misery I suffer comes from over-attention to my own self, and the troubles of the Empire from over-regulation in everything.' Thereupon, he threw up all his schemes, abandoned his ancestral palace, dismissed his attendants, removed all the hanging bells, cut down the delicacies of his *cuisine*, and retired to live at leisure in private apartments attached to the Court. There he fasted in heart, and brought his body under control.

Fasting in heart means freeing oneself from earthly desires, after which, says the commentator, the body will naturally be under control. Actual abstention from food or other forms of bodily mortification are not intended. See Musings of a *Chinese Mystic*, p. 71.

For three months he abstained from personal intervention in government. Then he fell asleep in the daytime, and dreamed that he made a journey to the kingdom of Hua-hsü, situated I know not how many tens of thousands of miles distant from the Ch'i State. It

23

was beyond the reach of ship or vehicle or any mortal foot. Only the soul could travel so far.

In sleep, the *hun* or spiritual part of the soul is supposed by the Chinese, to quit the body.

This kingdom was without head or ruler; it simply went on of itself. Its people were without desires or cravings; they simply followed their natural instincts. They felt neither joy in life nor abhorrence of death; thus they came to no untimely ends. They felt neither attachment to self nor indifference to others; thus they were exempt from love and hatred alike. They knew neither aversion from one course nor inclination to another; hence profit and loss existed not among them. All were equally untouched by the emotions of love and sympathy, of jealousy and fear. Water had no power to drown them, nor fire to burn; cuts and blows caused them neither injury nor pain, scratching or tickling could not make them itch. They bestrode the air as though treading on solid earth; they were cradled in space as though resting in a bed. Clouds and mist obstructed not their vision, thunder-peals could not stun their ears, physical beauty disturbed not their hearts, mountains and valleys hindered not their steps. They moved about like gods.

When the Yellow Emperor awoke from his dream, he summoned his three Ministers and told them what he had seen. 'For three months,' he said, 'I have been living a life of leisure, fasting in heart, subduing my body, and casting about in my mind for the true method of nourishing my own life and regulating the lives of others. But I failed to discover the secret.

'It is wrong to nourish one's own life, wrong to regulate those of others. No attempt to do this by the light of intelligence can be successful.'

Worn out, I fell asleep and dreamed this dream. Now I know that the Perfect Way is not to be sought through the senses. This Way I know and hold within me, yet I cannot impart it to you.'

'If the Way cannot be sought through the senses, it cannot be communicated through the senses.'

For twenty-eight years after this, there was great orderliness in the Empire, nearly equalling that in the kingdom of Hua-hsü. And when the Emperor ascended on high, the people bewailed him for two hundred years without intermission.

*   *   *

Lieh Tzu had Lao Shang for his teacher, and Po Kao Tzu for his friend. When he had fully mastered the system of these two philosophers, he rode home again on the wings of the wind.

Cf. *Chuang Tzu*, ch. 1: 'There was Lieh Tzu again. He could ride upon the wind, and travel whithersoever he wished, staying away as long as fifteen days.'

Yin Sheng heard of this, and became his disciple. He dwelt with Lieh Tzu for many months without Visiting his own home. While he was with him, he begged to be Initiated into his secret arts. Ten times he asked, and each time received no answer. Becoming impatient Yin Sheng announced his departure, but Lieh Tzu still gave no sign. So Yin Sheng went away, but after many months his mind was still unsettled, so he returned and became his follower once more. Lieh Tzu said to him: 'Why this incessant going and coming?' Yin Shêng replied: 'Some time ago, I sought instruction from you, Sir, but you would not tell me anything. That made me vexed with you. But now I have got rid of that feeling, and so I have come again.' Lieh Tzu said: 'Formerly, I used to think you were a man of penetration, and have you now fallen so low? Sit down, and I will tell you what I learned from my Master. After I had served him, and enjoyed the friendship of Po Kao, for the space of three years, my mind did not venture to reflect on right and my wrong, my lips did not venture to speak of profit and loss. Then, for the first time, my Master bestowed one glance upon me--and that was all.

'To be in reality entertaining the ideas of profit and loss, though without venturing to utter them, is a case of hiding one's resentment and harbouring secret passions; hence a mere glance was vouchsafed.'

25

'At the end of five years a change had taken place; my mind was reflecting on right and wrong, and my lips were speaking of profit and loss. Then, for the first time, my Master relaxed his countenance and smiled.

'Right and wrong, profit and loss, are the fixed principles prevailing in the world of sense. To let the mind reflect on what it will, to let the lips utter what they please, and not grudgingly bottle it up in one's breast, so that the internal and the external may become as one, is still not so good as passing beyond the bounds of self and abstaining from all manifestation. This first step, however, pleased the Master and caused him to give a smile.'

'At the end of seven years, there was another change. I let my mind reflect on what it would, but it no longer occupied itself with right and wrong. I let my lips utter whatsoever they pleased, but they no longer spoke of profit and loss. Then, at last, my Master led me in to sit on the mat beside him.

'The question is, how to bring the mind into a state of calm, in which there is no thinking or mental activity; how to keep the lips silent, with only natural inhalation and exhalation going on. If you give yourself up to mental perfection, right and wrong will cease to exist; if the lips follow their natural law they know not profit or loss. Their ways agreeing, Master and friend sat side by side with him on the same seat. That was only as it should be.'

'At the end of nine years my mind gave free rein to its reflections, my mouth free passage to its speech. Of right and wrong, profit and loss, I had no knowledge, either as touching myself or others. I knew neither that the Master was my instructor, nor that the other man was my friend. Internal and External were blended into Unity. After that, there was no distinction between eye and ear, ear and nose, nose and mouth: all were the same. My mind was frozen, my body in dissolution, my flesh and bones all melted together. I was wholly unconscious of what my body was resting on, or what was under my feet. I was borne this way and that on the wind, like dry chaff or leaves falling from a tree. In fact, I knew not whether the wind was riding on me or I on the wind. Now, you have not spent one whole season in your teacher's house, and yet you have lost patience two or three times already. Why, at this rate, the atmosphere will never support an atom of your body, and even the earth will be unequal to the weight of one of your limbs!

The only way to etherealize the body being to purge the mind of its passions.

How can you expect to walk in the void or to be charioted on the wind?'

Hearing this, Yin Sheng was deeply ashamed. He could hardly trust himself to breathe, and it was long ere he ventured to utter another word.

*   *   *

Mr Fan had a son named Tzu Hua, who succeeded in achieving great fame as an exponent of the black art, and the whole kingdom bowed down before him. He was in high favour with the Prince of Chin, taking no office but standing on a par with the three Ministers of State. Any one on whom he turned a partial eye was marked out for distinction; while those of whom he spoke unfavourably were forthwith banished. People thronged his hall in the same way as they went to Court. Tzu Hua used to encourage his followers to contend amongst themselves, so that the clever ones were always bullying the slowwitted, and the strong riding rough-shod over the weak. Though this resulted in blows and wounds being dealt before his eyes, he was not in the habit of troubling about it. Day and night, this sort of thing served as an amusement, and practically became a custom in the State.

One day, Ho Shêng and Tzu Po, two of Fan's leading disciples, set off on a journey and, after traversing a stretch of wild country, they put up for the night in the hut of an old peasant named Shang Ch'iu Wai. During the night, the two travellers conversed together, speaking of Tzu Hua's reputation and influence, his power over life and death, and how he could make the rich man poor and the poor man rich. Now, Shang Ch'iu Wai was living on the border of starvation. He had crept round under the window and overheard this conversation. Accordingly, he borrowed some provisions and, shouldering his basket, set off for Tzu Hua's establishment. This man's followers, however, were a worldly set, who wore silken garments and rode in high carriages and stalked about with their noses in the air. Seeing that Shang Ch'iu Wai was a weak old man, with a weather-beaten face and clothes of no particular cut, they one and all despised him. Soon he became a regular target for their insults and ridicule, being hustled about and slapped on the back and what not. Shang Ch'iu K'ai, however, never showed the least annoyance, and at last the disciples, having exhausted their wit on him in this way, grew tired of the fun. So, by way of a jest, they took the old man with them to the top of a cliff, and the word was passed round that whosoever dared to throw himself over would be rewarded with a hundred ounces of silver. There was an eager response, and Shang Ch'iu K'ai, in perfect good faith, was the first to leap over the edge. And lo! he was wafted down to earth like a bird on the wing, not a bone or muscle of his body being hurt. Mr Fan's disciples, regarding this as a lucky chance, were merely surprised, but not yet moved to great wonder. Then they pointed to a bend in the foaming river below, saying: 'There is a precious pearl at the bottom of that river, which can be had for the diving.' Ch'iu K'ai again acted on their suggestion and plunged in. And when he came out, sure enough he held a pearl in his hand.

Then, at last, the whole company began to suspect the truth, and Tzu Hua gave orders that an array of costly viands and silken raiment should be prepared; then suddenly a great fire was kindled round the pile. 'If you can walk through the midst of these flames,' he said, 'you are welcome to keep what you can get of these embroidered stuffs, be it much or little, as a reward.' Without moving a muscle of his face, Shang Ch'iu K'ai walked straight into the fire, and came back again with his garments unsoiled and his body unsinged.

Mr Fan and his disciples now realized that he was in possession of Tao, and all began to make their apologies, saying: 'We did not know, Sir, that you had Tao, and were only playing a trick on you. We insulted you, not knowing that you were a divine man. You have exposed our stupidity, our deafness and out blindness. May we venture to ask what the Great Secret is?' 'Secret I have none,' replied Shang Ch'iu K'ai. 'Even in my own mind I have no clue as to the real cause. Nevertheless, there is one point in it all which I must try to explain to you. A short time ago, Sir, two disciples of yours came and put up for the night in my hut. I heard them extolling Mr Fan's powers--how he could dispense life and death at his will, and how he was able to make the rich man poor and the poor man rich. I believed this implicitly, and as the distance was not very great I came hither. Having arrived, I unreservedly accepted as true all the statements made by your disciples, and was only afraid lest the opportunity might never come of putting them triumphantly to the proof I knew not what part of space my body occupied, nor yet where danger lurked. My mind was simply One, and material objects thus offered no resistance. That is all. But now, having discovered that your disciples were deceiving me, my inner man is thrown into a state of doubt and perplexity, while outwardly my senses of sight and hearing re-assert themselves. When I reflect that I have just had a providential escape from being drowned and burned to death, my heart within me freezes with horror, and my limbs tremble with fear. I shall never again have the courage to go near water or fire.'

From that time forth, when Mr Fan's disciples happened to meet a beggar or a poor horse-doctor on the road, so far from jeering at him, they would actually dismount and offer him a humble salute.

Tsai Wo heard this story, and told it to Confucius. 'Is this so strange to you? was the reply. 'The man of perfect faith can extend his influence to inanimate things and disembodied spirits; he can move heaven and earth, and fly to the six cardinal points without encountering any hindrance.

Compare the familiar passage in the Bible (Matt. xvii. 20).

His powers are not confined to walking in perilous places and passing through water and fire. If Shang Ch'iu K'ai, who put his faith in falsehoods, found no obstacle in external matter, how much more certainly will that be so when both parties are equally sincere! Young man, bear this in mind.'

In Shang Ch'iu K'ai's case, though he himself was sincere, his Master Fan Tzu Hua was merely an impostor.

* * *

The Keeper of Animals under King Hsüan, of the Chou dynasty, had an assistant named Liang Yang, who was skilled in the management of wild birds and beasts. When he fed them in their park-enclosure, all the animals showed themselves tame and tractable, although they comprised tigers, wolves, eagles and ospreys. Male and female freely propagated their kind, and their numbers multiplied.

The difficulty of getting wild animals to breed in captivity is well known to naturalists.

The different species lived promiscuously together, yet they never clawed nor bit one another.

The King was afraid lest this man's secret should die with him, and commanded him to impart it to the Keeper. So Liang Yang appeared before the Keeper and said: 'I am only a humble servant, and have really nothing to impart. I fear his Majesty thinks I am hiding something from you. With regard to my method of feeding tigers, all I have to say is this: when yielded to, they are pleased; when opposed, they are angry. Such is the natural disposition of all living creatures. But neither their pleasure nor their anger is manifested without a cause. Both are really excited by opposition.

Anger directly, pleasure indirectly, owing to the natural reaction when the opposition is overcome.

'In feeding tigers, then, I avoid giving them either live animals or whole carcases, lest in the former case the act of killing, in the latter the act of tearing them to pieces, should excite them to fury. Again, I

30

time their periods of hunger and repletion, and I gain a full understanding of the causes of their anger. Tigers are of a different species from man, but, like him, they respond to those who coax them with food, and consequently the act of killing their victims tends to provoke them. This being so, I should not think of opposing them and thus provoking their anger; neither do I humour them and thus cause them to feel pleased. For this feeling of pleasure will in time be succeeded by anger, just as anger must invariably be succeeded by pleasure. Neither of these states hits the proper mean. Hence it is my aim to be neither antagonistic nor compliant, so that the animals regard me as one of themselves. Thus it happens that they walk about the park without regretting the tall forests and the broad marshes, and rest in the enclosure without yearning for the lonely mountains and the dark valleys. Such are the principles which have led to the results you see.'

* * *

There was once a man, a sailor by profession, who was very fond of sea-gulls. Every morning he went into the sea and swam about in their midst, at which times a hundred gulls and more would constantly flock about him.

'Creatures are not shy of those whom they feel to be in mental and bodily harmony with themselves.'

One day his father said to him: 'I am told that sea-gulls swim about with you in the water. I wish you would catch one or two for me to make pets of' On the following day, the sailor went down to the sea as usual, but lo! the gulls only wheeled about in the air and would not alight.

'There was disturbance in his mind, accompanied by a change in his outward demeanour; thus the birds became conscious of the fact that he was a human being. How could their instinct be deceived?'

* * *

Chao Hsiang Tzu led out a company of a hundred thousand men to hunt in the Central Mountains. Lighting the dry undergrowth, they set fire to the whole forest, and the glow of the flames was visible for a hundred miles around. Suddenly a man appeared, emerging from a rocky cliff,

That is to say, passing miraculously out of the actual stone itself.

and was seen to hover in the air amidst the flames and the smoke. Everybody took him for a disembodied spirit. When the fire had passed, he walked quietly out, and showed no trace of having been through the ordeal. Hsiang Tzu marvelled thereat, and detained him for the purpose of careful examination. In bodily form he was undoubtedly a man, possessing the seven channels of sense, besides which his breathing and his voice also proclaimed him a man. So the prince inquired what secret power it was that enabled him to dwell in rock and to walk through fire. 'What do you mean by rock? replied the man; 'what do you mean by fire? Hsiang Tzu said: 'What you just now came out of is rock; what you just how walked through is fire.' 'I know nothing of them,' replied the man.

'It was this extreme feat of unconsciousness that enabled him to perform the above feats.'

The incident came to the ears of Marquis Wên of the Wei State, who spoke to Tzu Hsia about it, saying: 'What an extraordinary man this must be!' 'From what I have heard the Master say,' replied Tzu Hsia, 'the man who achieves harmony with Tao enters into close unison with external objects, and none of them has the power to harm or hinder him. Passing through solid metal or stone, walking in the midst of fire or on the surface of water--all these things become possible to him.' 'Why, my friend,' asked the Marquis, 'cannot you do all this? 'I have not yet succeeded,' said Tzu Hsia, 'in cleansing my heart of impurities and discarding Wisdom. I can only find leisure to discuss the matter in tentative fashion.' 'And why,' pursued the Marquis, 'does not the Master himself perform these feats? 'The Master,' replied Tzu' Hsia, 'is is able to do these things, but he is also able to refrain from doing them.' Which answer hugely delighted the Marquis.

There may be similarity in understanding without similarity in outward form. There may also be similarity in form without similarity in understanding. The Sage embraces similarity of understanding and pays no regard to similarity of form. The world in general is attracted by similarity of form, but remains indifferent to similarity of understanding. Those creatures that resemble them in shape they love and consort with; those that differ from them in shape they fear and keep at a distance. The creature that has a skeleton seven feet long,

The Chinese foot at that time being considerably shorter than ours.

hands differently shaped from the feet, hair on its head, and an even set of teeth in its jaws, and walks erect, is called a man. But it does not follow that a man may not have the mind of a brute. Even though this be the case, other men will still recognize him as one of their own species in virtue of his outward form. Creatures which have wings on the back or horns on the head, serrated teeth or extensile talons, which fly overhead or run on all fours, are called birds and beasts. But it does not follow that a bird or a beast may not have the mind of a man. Yet, even if this be so, it is nevertheless assigned to another species because of the difference in form.

P'ao Hsi, Nü Kua, Shên Nung and Hsia Hou had serpents' bodies, human faces, ox-heads and tigers' snouts. Thus, their forms were not human, yet their virtue was of the saintliest. Chieh of the Hsia dynasty, Chou of the Yin, Huan of the Lu State, and Mu of the Ch'u State, were in all external respects, as facial appearance and Possession of the seven channels of sense, like unto other men; yet they had the minds of savage brutes. Howbeit, in seeking perfect understanding, men attend to the outward form alone, which will not bring them near to it.

When the Yellow Emperor fought with Yen Ti on the field of P'an-ch'üan, his vanguard was composed of bears, wolves, panthers, lynxes and tigers, while his ensign-bearers were eagles, ospreys, falcons and kites. This was forcible impressment of animals into the service of man. The Emperor Yao entrusted K'uei with the regulation of music.

K'uei was a composite being, half beast, half man, of irreproachable virtue. His son, on the other hand, is said to have had 'the heart of a pig'. He was insatiably gluttonous, covetous and quarrelsome.

When the latter tapped the musical stone in varying cadence, all the animals danced to the sound of the music. When the *Shao* in its nine variations was heard on the flute, the phœnix itself flew down to assist. This was the attraction of animals by the power of music. In what, then, do the minds of birds and beasts differ from the minds of men? Their shapes and the sounds they utter are different from ours, and they know no way of communicating with us. But the wisdom and penetration of the Sage are unlimited: that is why he is able to lead then, to do his bidding. The intelligence of animals is innate, even as that of man. Their common desire is for self-preservation, but they do not borrow their knowledge from men. There is pairing between the male and the female, and mutual attachment between the mother and her young. They shun the open plain and keep to the mountainous parts; they flee the cold and make for warmth; when they settle, they gather in flocks; when they travel, they preserve a fixed order. The young ones are stationed in the middle, the stronger ones place themselves on the outside. They show one another the way to the drinking-places, and call to their fellows when there is food. In the earliest ages, they dwelt and moved about in company with man. It was not until the age of emperors and kings that they began to be afraid and broke away into scattered bands. And now, in this final period, they habitually hide and keep out of man's way so as to avoid injury at his hands. At the present day, in the country of the Chieh clan to the east, the people can often interpret the language of the six domestic animals, although they have probably but an imperfect understanding of it.

In remote antiquity, there were men of divine enlightenment who were perfectly acquainted with the feelings and habits of all living things, and thoroughly understood the languages of the various species. They brought them together, trained them, and admitted them to their society, exactly like human beings....These sages declared that, in mind and understanding, there was no wide gulf between any of the living species endowed with blood and breath. And therefore, knowing that this was so, they omitted nothing from their course of training and instruction.

*   *   *

Hui Yang went to visit Prince K'ang of the Sung State. The Prince, however, stamped his foot, rasped his throat, and said angrily: 'The things I like are courage and strength. I am not fond of your good and virtuous people. What can a stranger like you have to teach me? 'I have a secret,' replied Hui Yang, 'whereby my opponent, however brave or strong, can be prevented from harming me either by thrust or by blow. Would not your Highness care to know that secret? 'Capital!' exclaimed K'ang; 'that is certainly something I should like to hear about.' Hui Yang went on: 'To render ineffectual the stabs and blows of one's opponent is indeed to cover him with shame. But my secret is one which will make your opponent, however brave or strong, afraid to stab or to strike at all! His being afraid, however, does not always imply that he has not the will to do so. Now, my secret method operates so that even the will is absent. Not having the will to harm, however, does not necessarily connote the desire to love and to do good. But my secret is one whereby every man, woman and child in the Empire shall be inspired with the friendly desire to love and do good to one another! This is something that transcends all social distinctions, and is much better than the mere possession of courage and strength. Has your Highness no mind to acquire such a secret as this?' 'Nay,' said the Prince, 'I am anxious to learn it. What is the secret, pray?' 'Nothing else,' replied Hui Yang, 'than the teachings of Confucius and Mo Tzu.

A famous philosopher who flourished about 400 B.C. and propounded, chiefly on utilitarian grounds, the doctrine of 'universal love'.

Neither of these two men possessed any land, and yet they were princes; they held no official rank, and yet they were leaders. All the inhabitants of the Empire, old and young, used to crane their necks and stand on tiptoe to catch a glimpse of them. For it was their object to bring peace and happiness to all. Now, your Highness is lord of ten thousand chariots.

A conventional way of saying that Swig was a feudal State of the first class.

If you are sincere in your purpose, all the people within the four borders of your realm will reap the benefit, and the fame of your virtue will far exceed that of Confucius or of Mo Tzu.'

They not having enjoyed the advantage of ruling over a large State.

The Prince of Sung found himself at loss for an answer, and Hui Yang quickly withdrew. Then the Prince turned to his courtiers and said: 'A forcible argument! This stranger has carried me away by his eloquence.'

Book III - Dreams

In the time of King Mu of Chou, there was a magician who came from a kingdom in the far west. He could pass through fire and water, penetrate metal and stone, overturn mountains and make rivers flow backwards, transplant whole towns and cities, ride on thin air without falling, encounter solid bodies without being obstructed. There was no end to the countless variety of changes and transformations which he could effect; and, besides changing the external form, he could also spirit away men's internal cares.

King Mu revered him as a god, and served him like a prince. He set aside for his use a spacious suite of apartments, regaled him with the daintiest of food, and selected a number of singing-girls for his express gratification. The magician, however, condemned the King's palace as mean, the cooking as rancid, and the concubines as too ugly to live with. So King Mu had a new building erected to please him. It was built entirely of bricks and wood, and gorgeously decorated in red and white, no skill being spared in its construction. The five royal treasuries were empty by the time that the new pavilion was complete. It stood six thousand feet high, overtopping Mount Chung-nan, and it was called Touch-the-sky Pavilion. Then the King proceeded to fill it with maidens, selected from Chêng and Wei, of the most exquisite and delicate beauty. They were anointed with fragrant perfumes, adorned with moth-eyebrows, provided with jewelled hairpins and earrings, and arrayed in the finest silks, with costly satin trains. Their faces were powdered, and their eyebrows pencilled, their girdles were studded with precious stones. All manner of sweet-scented plants filled the palace with their odours, and ravishing music of the olden time was played to the honoured guest. Every month he was presented with fresh and costly raiment; every morning he had set before him some new and delicious food.

The magician could not well refuse to take up his abode in this palace of delight. But he had not dwelt there very long before he invited the King to accompany him on a jaunt. So the King clutched the magician's sleeve, and soared up with him higher and higher into the sky, until at last they stopped, and lo! they had reached the magician's own palace. This palace was built with beams of gold and silver, and incrusted with pearls and jade. It towered high above the region of clouds and rain, and the foundations whereon it rested were unknown. It appeared like a stupendous cloud-mass to the view. The sights and sounds it offered to eye and ear, the scents and flavours which abounded there, were such as exist not within mortal ken. The King verily believed that he was in the Halls of Paradise, tenanted by God Himself, and that he was listening to the mighty music of the spheres. He gazed at his own palace on the earth below, and it seemed to him no better than a rude pile of clods and brushwood.

It seemed to the King as if his stay in this place lasted for several decades, during which he gave no thought to his own kingdom. Then the magician invited him to make another journey, and in the new region they came to, neither sun nor moon could be seen in the heavens above, nor any rivers or seas below. The King's eyes were dazed by the quality of the light, and he lost the power of vision; his ears were stunned by the sounds that assailed them, and he lost the faculty of hearing. The framework of his bones and his internal organs were thrown out of gear and refused to function. His thoughts were in a whirl, his intellect became clouded, and he begged the

'This was the region of the Great Void, where all is dim and blurred, assuredly not meant to be traversed by the ordinary man. The dizziness of brain and eye was the effect produced by the Absolute.'

magician to take him back again. Thereupon, the magician gave him a shove, and the King experienced a sensation of falling through space....

When he awoke to consciousness, he found himself sitting on his throne just as before, with the selfsame attendants round him. He looked at the wine in front of him, and saw that it was still full of sediment; he looked at the viands, and found that they had not yet lost their freshness. He asked where he had come from, and his attendants told him that he had only been sitting quietly there. This threw King Mu into a reverie, and it was three months before he was himself again. Then he made further inquiry, and asked the magician to explain what had happened. 'Your Majesty and I, 'replied the magician, 'were only wandering about in the spirit, and, of course, our bodies never moved at all. What essential difference is there between that sky-palace we dwelt in and your Majesty's palace on earth, between the spaces we travelled through and your Majesty's own park?

Looked at from the standpoint of the Absolute, both palaces were unreal.

You are accustomed to being permanently in the body, and cannot understand being out of it for a while. Can any number of changes, or successive intervals of fast and slow, fully represent the true scheme of things?'

The King was much pleased. He ceased to worry about affairs of State, and took no further pleasure in the society of his ministers or concubines.

The sky-palace was only some degrees finer than the King's, just as the King's palace was only some degrees finer than the hovel of a peasant. To strive for something that shall satisfy man's desires and aspirations once and for all is only labour lost. The story continues with an account of the King's marvellous journey to the West. But though he drained the cup of pleasure to the dregs, the upshot of it all was that he never truly attained to Tao. We may seek the moral in a saying of Lao Tzu: 'Without going out of doors, one may know the whole world; without looking out of window, one may see the Way of Heaven. The farther one travels, the less one may know.'

Lao Ch'êng Tzu went to learn magic from the venerable Yin Wên. After a period of three years, having obtained no communication, he humbly asked permission to go home. Yin Wên bowed, and led him into the inner apartment. There, having dismissed his attendants, he spoke to him as follows: 'Long ago, when Lao Tzu was setting out on his journey to the West, he addressed me and said: "All that has the breath of life, all that possesses bodily form, is mere illusion. The point at which creation begins, the change effected by the Dual Principles--these are called respectively Life and Death. That which underlies the manifold workings of Destiny is called Evolution; that which produces and transforms bodily substance is called Illusion. The ingenuity of the Creative Power is mysterious, and its operations are profound. In truth, it is inexhaustible and eternal.

The 'Creative Power', of course, is Tao; but how widely the conception of Tao, differs from that of a personal God may be seen from the commentator's note: 'How should the Creative Power possess a conscious mind? It is its spontaneity that constitutes the mystery. Spirit and matter eagerly come together and coalesce into perceptible forms. Following the path of evolution they proceed on their way, and before long relapse into nothingness.'

The ingenuity of that which causes material form is patent to the eye, and its operations are superficial. Therefore it arises anon, and anon it vanishes." Only one who knows that Life is really Illusion, and that Death is really Evolution, can begin to learn magic from me. You and I are both illusions. What need, then, to make a study of the subject?

'If a person wishes to make a study of illusion, in spite of the fact that his own body is an illusion, we are reduced to the absurdity of an illusion studying an illusion.'

Lao Ch'êng Tzu returned home, and for three months pondered deeply over the words of the Venerable Yin Wên. Subsequently, he had the power of appearing or disappearing at will; he could reverse the order of the four seasons, produce thunderstorms in winter and ice in summer, make flying things creep and creeping things fly. But to the end of his days he never published the secret of his art, so that it was not handed down to after generations.

*　　*　　*

The Master Lieh Tzu said: 'A dream is something that comes into contact with the mind; an external event is something that impinges on the body. Hence our feelings by day and our dreams by night are the result of contacts made by mind or body. it follows that if we can concentrate the maid in abstraction, our feelings and our dreams will vanish of themselves. Those who rely on their waking perceptions will not argue about them. Those who put faith in dreams do not understand the processes of change in the external world.

This refers to a previous passage, omitted in the present selection. Contrary to the received opinion of his own day, Lieh Tzu held that dreams were not just arbitrary manifestations portending future events, but the effects of regular antecedent causes, without any further significance. They are produced by certain processes of the mind, and if these processes can be checked (as Lieh Tzu believes they can) by means of abstraction, dreaming will also cease.

"The pure men of old passed their waking existence in self-oblivion, and slept without dreams." How can this be dismissed as an empty phrase?

*　　*　　*

Mr Yin of Chou was the owner of a large estate who harried his servants unmercifully, and gave them no rest from morning to night. There was one old servant in particular whose physical strength had quite left him, yet his master worked him all the harder. All day long he was groaning as he went about his work, and when night came he was reeling with fatigue and would sleep like a

41

log. His spirit was then free to wander at will, and every night he dreamt that he was a king, enthroned in authority over the multitude, and controlling the affairs of the whole State. He took his Pleasure in palaces and belvederes, following his own fancy in everything, and his happiness was beyond compare. But when he awoke, he was servant once more. To some one who condoled with him on his hard lot the old man replied: 'Human life may last a hundred years, and the whole of it is equally divided into nights and days. In the daytime I am only a slave, it is true, and my misery cannot be gainsaid. But by night I am a king, and my happiness is beyond compare. So what have I to grumble at?'

Now, Mr Yin's mind was full of worldly cares, and he was always thinking with anxious solicitude about the affairs of his estate. Thus he was wearing out mind and body alike, and at night he also used to fall asleep utterly exhausted. Every night he dreamt that he was another man's servant, running about on menial business; of every description, and subjected to every possible kind of abuse and ill-treatment. He would mutter and groan in his sleep, and obtained no relief until morning came. This state of things at last resulted in a serious illness, and Mr Yin besought the advice of a friend. 'Your station in life,' his friend said, 'is a distinguished one, and you have wealth and property in abundance. In these respects you are far above the average. If at night you dream that you are a servant and exchange ease for affliction, that is only the proper balance in human destiny. What you want is that your dreams should be as pleasant as your waking moments. But that is beyond your power to compass.' On hearing what his friend said, Mr Yin lightened his servant's toil, and allowed his own mental worry to abate; whereupon his malady began to decrease in proportion.

*   *   *

A man was gathering fuel in the Cheng State when he fell in with a deer that had been startled from its usual haunts. He gave chase, and succeeded in killing it. He was overjoyed at his good luck; but, for fear of discovery, he hastily concealed the carcass in a dry ditch, and covered it up with brushwood. Afterwards, he forgot the spot where he had hidden the deer, and finally became convinced that the whole affair was only a dream. He told the story to people he met as he went along; and one of those who heard it, following the indications given, went and found the deer. On reaching home with his booty, this man made the following statement to his wife: 'Once upon a time,' he said, 'a wood-cutter dreamt that he had got a deer, but couldn't remember the place where he had put it. Now I have found the deer, so it appears that his dream was a true dream.' 'On the contrary.' said his wife, 'it is you who must have dreamt that you met a wood-cutter who had caught a deer. Here you have a deer, true enough. But where is the wood-cutter? it is evidently your dream that has come true.' 'I have certainly got a deer,' replied her husband; 'so what does it matter to us whether it was his dream or mine?'

Meanwhile, the wood-cutter had gone home, not at all disgusted at having lost the deer.

For he thought the whole thing must have been a dream.

But the same night, he saw in a dream the place where he had really hidden it, and he also dreamt of the man who had taken it. So, the next morning, in accordance With his dream, he went to seek him out in order to recover the deer. A quarrel ensued, and the matter was finally brought before the magistrate, who gave judgment in these terms: 'You,' he said to the wood-cutter, 'began by really killing a deer, but wrongly thought it was a dream. Then you really dreamt that you had got the deer, but wrongly took the dream to be a reality. The other man really took your deer, which he is now disputing with you. His wife, on the other hand, declares that he saw both man and deer in a dream, so that nobody can be said to have killed the deer at all. Meanwhile, here is the deer itself in court, and you had better divide it between you.'

The case was reported to the Prince of the Chêng State, who said: 'Why, the magistrate must have dreamt the whole thing himself!' The question was referred to the Prime Minister, but the latter confessed himself unable to disentangle the part that was a dream from that part that was not a dream. 'If you want to distinguish between waking and dreaming,' he said, 'only the Yellow Emperor or Confucius could help you. But both these sages are dead, and there is nobody now alive who can draw any such distinction.

Of course, it is implied that there *is* no real distinction between the two.

So the best thing you can do is to uphold the magistrate's decision.'

*   *   *

Yang-li Hua-tzü, of the Sung State, was afflicted in middle age by loss of memory. Anything he received in the morning he had forgotten by the evening, anything he gave away in the evening he had forgotten the next morning. Out-of-doors, he forgot to walk; indoors, he forgot to sit down. At any given moment, he had no recollection of what had just taken place; and a little later on, he could not even recollect what had happened then. All his family were perfectly disgusted with him. Fortune-tellers were summoned, but their divinations proved unsuccessful; Wizards were sought out, but their exorcisms were ineffectual; physicians were called in, but their remedies were of no avail. At last, a learned professor from the Lu State volunteered his services, declaring that he could effect a cure. Hua-tzu's wife and family immediately offered him half their estate if only he would tell them how to set to work. The professor replied: 'This is a case which cannot be dealt with by means of auspices and diagrams; the evil cannot be removed by prayers and incantations, nor successfully combated by drugs and potions. What I shall try to do is to influence his mind and turn the current of his thoughts; in that way a cure is likely to be brought about.'

Accordingly, the experiment was begun. The professor exposed his patient to cold, so that he was forced to beg for clothes; subjected him to hunger, so that he was fain to ask for food; left him in darkness, so that he was obliged to search for light. Soon, he was able to report progress to the sons of the house, saying gleefully:

44

'The disease can be checked. But the methods I shall employ have been handed down as a secret in my family, and cannot be made known to the public. All attendants must, therefore, be kept out of the way, and I must be shut up alone with my patient.' The professor was allowed to have his way, and for the space of seven days no one knew what was going on in the sick man's chamber. Then, one fine morning, the treatment came to an end, and, wonderful to relate, the disease of so many years' standing had entirely disappeared!

No sooner had Hua-tzu regained his senses, however, than he flew into a great rage, drove his wife out of doors, beat his sons, and, snatching up a spear, hotly pursued the professor through the town. On being arrested and asked to explain his conduct, this is what he said: 'Lately when I was steeped in forgetfulness, my senses were so benumbed that I was quite unconscious of the existence of the outer world. But now I have been brought suddenly to a perception of the events of half a lifetime. Preservation and destruction, gain and loss, sorrow and joy, love and hate have begun to throw out their myriad tentacles to invade my peace; and these emotions will, I fear, continue to keep my mind in the state of turmoil that I now experience. Oh! if I could but recapture a short moment of that blesséd oblivion!'

'If such is the man's reaction to an infirmity which resembles the Highest Principle, how much greater will be the effect of incorporation in the Absolute!'

*   *   *

There was once a man who, though born in Yen, was brought up in Ch'u, and it was only in his old age that he returned to his native country.

Yen was the northernmost State of ancient China, while Ch'u was bounded by the left bank of the Yangtsze.

On the way thither, as they were passing through the Chin State, a fellow-traveller played a practical joke on him. Pointing to the city he said: 'Here is the capital of the Yen State'; whereupon the old man flushed with excitement. Pointing out a certain shrine, he told him that it was his own village altar, and the old man heaved a deep sigh. Then he showed him a house, and said: 'This is where your ancestors lived'; and the tears welled up in his eyes. Finally, a mound was pointed out to him as the tomb where his ancestors lay buried, whereupon the old man could control himself no longer, and wept aloud. But his fellow-traveller burst into roars of laughter. 'I have been hoaxing you,' he cried; 'this is only the Chin State.' His victim was greatly mortified; and when he arrived at his journey's end, and really did see before him the city and altars of Yen, with the actual abode and tombs of his ancestors. his emotion was much less acute.

Book IV - Confucius

A high official from Shang paid a visit to Confucius 'You are a sage, are you not? he inquired. 'A sage! replied Confucius. 'How could I venture to think so? I am only a man with a wide range of learning and information.' The Minister then asked: 'Were the Three Kings sages?

The Three Kings, in this particular passage, are probably T'ang, surnamed 'The Completer' or 'The Successful', who founded the Shang dynasty, 1766 B.C., and the two founders of the Chou dynasty, Wên and Wu. The word *shêng*, here translated 'sage', implies a man inspired by Heaven.

'The Three Kings,' replied Confucius, 'were great in the exercise of wisdom and courage. I do not know, however, that they were sages.' 'What of the Five Emperors? Were they not sages?

Shao Hao, Chuan Hsü, Yao, Shun, and the Great Yü. The last-named came to the throne in 2205 B.C.

'The Five Emperors excelled in the exercise of altruism and righteousness. I do not know that they were sages.' 'And the Three Sovereigns: surely they were sages?

The Three Sovereigns always denote the legendary rulers Fu Hsi, Shên Nung and the Yellow Emperor.

'The Three Sovereigns excelled in the virtues that were suited to their age. But whether they were sages or no I really cannot say.'

'The wide learning of Confucius, the warlike prowess of T'ang and Wu, the humility and self-abnegation of Yao, and shun, the rude simplicity of Fu Hsi and Shên Nung, simply represent the ordinary activities of the sage who accommodates himself to the necessities of the world he lives in. They are not the qualities which make them sages. Those qualities are truly such as neither word nor deed can adequately express.

Why, who is there, then,' cried the Minister, much astonished, 'that is really a sage?' The expression of Confucius' countenance changed, and he replied after a pause: 'Among the people of the West a true sage dwells. He governs not, yet there is no disorder. He speaks not, yet he is naturally trusted. He makes no reforms, yet right conduct is spontaneous and universal. So great and incomprehensible is he that the people can find no name to call him by. I suspect that this man is a sage, but whether in truth he is a sage or is not a sage I do not know.'

The early Jesuit missionaries saw in the above an allusion to Jesus Christ. But (apart from other considerations) it is almost certain that the present work had taken definite shape before the Christian era. On the other hand, it is quite possible that the Sage whom Lieh Tzu had in mind was Sâkyamuni Buddha.

The Minister from Shang meditated awhile in silence. Then he said to himself: 'Confucius is making a fool of me!'

When the Master Lieh Tzu took up his abode in Nan-kuo the number of those who settled down with him was past reckoning, though one were to count them day by day. Lieh Tzu, however, continued to live in retirement, and every morning would hold discussions with them, the fame of which spread far and wide.

Nan-kuo Tzu was his next-door neighbour, but for twenty years no visit passed between them, and when they met in the street they made as though they had not seen each other.

'There was a mysterious harmony between their doctrines, and therefore they arrived at old age without having had any mutual intercourse.' Nan-kuo Tzu means simply 'the Philosopher of Nan-kuo'.

Lieh Tzu's disciples felt convinced that there was enmity between their Master and Nan-kuo Tzu; and at last, one who had come from the Ch'u State spoke to Lieh Tzu about it, saying: 'How comes it, Sir, that you and Nan-kuo Tzu are enemies? 'Nan-kuo

Tzu,' replied the Master, 'has the appearance of fullness, but his mind is a blank.

By no means a term of disparagement, in the mouth of a Taoist.

His ears do not hear, his eyes do not see, his mouth does not speak, his mind is devoid of knowledge, his body free from agitation. What would be the object of visiting him? However, we will try, and you shall accompany me thither to see.' Accordingly, forty of the disciples went with him to call on Nan-kuo Tzu, who turned out to be a repulsive-looking creature with whom they could make no contact.

Taoist writers seem to delight in attributing ugliness and deformity to their sages, no doubt as a sort of foil or set-off to their inward grandeur.

He only gazed blankly at Lieh Tzu. Mind and body seemed not to belong together, and his guests could find no means of approach.

'The soul had subjugated the body. The mind being void of sense-impressions, the countenance remained motionless. Hence it seemed as if there were no co-operation between the two. How could they respond to external stimuli?'

Suddenly, Nan-kuo Tzu singled out the hindermost row of Lieh Tzu's disciples, and began to talk to them quite pleasantly and simply, though in the tone of a superior.

'Fraternizing with the hindmost row, he recognized no distinctions of rank or standing; meeting a sympathetic influence, and responding thereto, he did not allow his mind to be occupied with the external.'

The disciples were astonished at this, and when they got home again, all wore a puzzled expression. Their Master Lieh Tzu said to them: 'He who has reached the stage of thought is silent. He who has attained to perfect knowledge is also silent. He who uses silence in lieu of speech really does speak. He who for knowledge substitutes blankness of mind really does know. Without words and speaking not, without knowledge and knowing not, he really speaks and really knows. Saying nothing and knowing nothing, there is in reality nothing that he does not say, nothing that he does not know. This is how the matter stands, and there is nothing further to be said. Why are you thus astonished without cause?'

*   *   *

Lung Shu said to Wên Chih:

'Wên Chih lived in the time of the Six States, and acted as physician to Prince Wei of Ch'i (378-333 B.C.]. Another account says that he was an able physician of the Sung State in the "Spring and Autumn" period, and that he cured Prince Wen of Ch'i by making him angry, whereupon his sickness vanished.'

'You are the master of cunning arts. I have a disease. Can you cure it, Sir? 'I am at your service,' replied Wên Chih. 'But please let me know first the symptoms of your disease.' 'I hold it no honour, said Lung Shu, 'to be praised in my native village, nor do I consider it a disgrace to he decried in my native State. Gain excites in me no joy, and loss no sorrow. I look upon life in the same light as death, upon riches in the same light as poverty, upon my fellow-men as so many swine, and upon myself as I look upon my fellow-men. I dwell in my home as though it were a mere caravanserai, and regard my native district with no more feeling than I would a barbarian State. Afflicted as I am in these various ways, honours and rewards fail to rouse me, pains and penalties to overawe me, good or bad fortune to influence me, joy or grief to move me. Thus I am incapable of serving my sovereign, of associating with my friends and kinsmen, of directing my wife and children, or of controlling my servants and retainers.

'Men are controlled by external influences in so far as their minds are open to impressions of good and evil, and their bodies are sensitive to injury or the reverse. But one who is able to discern a connecting unity in the most multiform diversity will surely, in his survey of the universe, be unconscious of the differences between positive and negative.'

What disease is this, and what remedy is there that will cure it?'

Wên Chih replied by asking Lung Shu to stand with his back to the light, while he himself faced the light and looked at him intently. 'Ah!' said he after a while, 'I see that a good square inch of your heart is hollow. You are within an ace of being a true sage. Six of the orifices in your heart are open and clear, and only the seventh is blocked up.

'It was an ancient belief that the sage had seven orifices in his heart' (the seat of the understanding).

This, however, is doubtless due to the fact that you are mistaking for a disease that which is really divine enlightenment. It is a case in which my shallow art is of no avail.'

*   *   *

Pu-tsê, in the Cheng State, was rich in wise men, and Tung-li in men of administrative talent. Among the vassals of Pu-tsê was a certain Po Fêng Tzu, who happened to travel through Tung-li and had a meeting with Têng Hsi.

A noted sophist of the sixth century B.C.

The latter cast a glance at his followers, and asked them, with a smile: 'Would you like to see me have some sport with this stranger? They understood what he would be at, and assented. Têng Hsi then turned to Po Fêng Tzu. 'Are you acquainted with the true theory of Sustentation? he inquired. 'To receive sustenance from others, through inability to support oneself, places one in the category of dogs and swine. It is man's prerogative to give sustenance to other creatures, and to use them for his own purposes. That you and your fellows are provided with abundant food and comfortable clothing is due to us administrators. Young and old, you herd together, and are penned up like cattle destined for the shambles: in what respect are you to be distinguished from dogs and swine?

Po Fêng Tzu made no reply, but one of his company, disregarding the rules of precedence, stepped forward and said: 'Has your Excellency never heard of the variety of craftsmen in Ch'i and Lu? Some are skilled potters and carpenters, others are clever workers in

51

metal and leather; there are good musicians, trained scribes and accountants, military experts and men learned in the ritual of ancestor-worship. All kinds of talent are there fully represented. But without proper organization, these craftsmen cannot be usefully employed. But those who organize them lack knowledge, those who employ them lack technical ability, and therefore they make use of those who have both knowledge and ability.

'Whoso possesses skill and knowledge of any particular kind is incapable of helping his prince in the direction of affairs!

So it is really *we* who may be said to employ the Government administrators. What is it, then, that you are boasting about?

Têng Hsi could think of nothing to say in reply. He glanced round at his disciples and retreated.

Book V - The Questions of Pang

T'ang of Yin questioned Hsia Ko, saying: 'In the beginnings of antiquity, did individual things exist?'

'He suspected that there was only Chaos, and nothing more.

'If things did not exist then,' replied Hsia Ko, 'how could they be in existence now? Or will the men of future ages be right in denying the existence of things at the present time?

'Things in that case,' pursued T'ang, 'have no before nor after?'

Hsia Ko replied: 'To the beginning and end of things there is no precise limit. Beginning may be end, and end may be beginning. How can we conceive of any fixed period to either?

'That which we call an end at the present moment may be the beginning of a new thing, and that which we call a beginning may, contrariwise, be the end of something. End and beginning succeed one another until at last they cannot be distinguished.'

But when it comes to something outside matter in space, or anterior to events in time, our knowledge fails us.'

'Then upwards and downwards and in every direction space is a finite quantity?

Ko replied: 'I do not know.'

'It was not so much that he did not know as that it is unknowable.'

T'ang asked the question again with more insistence, and Ko said: 'If there is nothing in space, then it is infinite; if there is something, then that something must have limits. How can I tell which is true? But beyond infinity there must again exist non-infinity, and within the unlimited again that which is not unlimited.

Lieh Tzu means that in this universe of relativity there must be contraries, even to a negative. We are only brought back, however, to our starting-point, for, as the commentator points out, that which is not infinite and not unlimited really stands for that which is finite and limited.

It is this consideration--that infinity must be succeeded by non-infinity, and the unlimited by the not-unlimited--that enables me to apprehend the infinity and unlimited extent of space, but does not allow me to conceive of its being finite and limited.'

*　　*　　*

T'ang continued his inquiries, saying: 'What is there beyond the Four Seas?

That is, the inhabited world as known to the Chinese.

Ko replied: 'Just what there is here in the province of Ch'i.'

'How can you prove that?' asked T'ang.

'When travelling eastwards,' said Ko, 'I came to the land of Ying, where the inhabitants were nowise different from those in this part of the country. I inquired about the countries east of Ying, and found that they, too, were similar to their neighbour. Travelling westwards, I came to Pin, where the inhabitants were similar to our own countrymen. I inquired about the countries west of Pin, and found that they were again similar to Pin. That is how I know that the regions within the Four Seas, the Four Wildernesses and the Four Uttermost Ends of the Earth are nowise different from the country we ourselves inhabit. Thus, the lesser is always enclosed by a greater, without ever reaching an end. Heaven and earth, which enclose the myriad objects of creation, are themselves enclosed in some outer shell.

'That which contains heaven and earth is the Great Void.'

Enclosing heaven and earth and the myriad objects within them, this outer shell is infinite and immeasurable. How do we know but that there is some mightier universe in existence outside our own? That is a question to which we can give no answer.

'Heaven and earth, then, are themselves only material objects, and therefore imperfect. Hence it is that Kua of old fashioned many-coloured blocks of stone to repair the defective parts.

'Nü Kua, being a divine man, was able to refine and extract the essence of the five constituents of matter!

He cut off the legs of the *Ao* and used them to support the four corners of the heavens.

This Chinese 'Atlas' was a gigantic sea-turtle.

Later on, Kung Kung fought with Chuan Hsü for the throne, and, blundering in his rage against Mount Pu-chou, he snapped the pillar which connects Heaven and earth.

At the north-western comer.

That is why Heaven dips downwards to the north-west, so that sun, moon and stars travel towards that quarter. The earth, on the other hand, is now not large enough to fill up the south-east, so that all rivers and streams roll in that direction.'

An ingenious theory to account for the apparent westward revolution of the heavenly bodies, as also for the easterly trend of the great Chinese rivers.

*　　*　　*

The two mountains T'ai-hsing and Wang-wu, which cover an area of 700 square *li*, and rise to an enormous altitude, originally stood in the south of the Chi district and north of Ho-yang. The Simpleton of the North Mountain, an old man of ninety, dwelt opposite these mountains, and was vexed in spirit because their northern flanks blocked the way to travellers, who had to go all the way round. So he called his family together, and broached a plan. 'Let us,' he said, 'put forth our utmost strength to clear away this obstacle, and cut right through the mountains until we come to Han-yin. What say you? They all assented except his wife, who made objections and said: 'My goodman has not the strength to sweep away a dunghill, let alone two such mountains as T'ai-hsing and Wang-wu. Besides, where will you put all the earth and stones that you dig up? The others replied that they would throw them on the promontory of P'o-hai. So the old man, followed by his son and grandson, sallied forth with their pickaxes, and the three of them began hewing away at the rocks, and cutting up the soil, and carting it away in baskets to the promontory of P'o-hai. A widowed woman who lived near had a little boy who, though he was only just shedding his milk teeth, came skipping along to give them what help he could. Engrossed in their toil, they never went home except once at the turn of the season.

The Wise Old Man of the River-bend burst out laughing and urged them to stop. 'Great indeed is your witlessness!' he said. 'With the poor remaining strength of your declining years you will not succeed in removing a hair's breadth of the mountain, much less the whole vast mass of rock and soil.' With a sigh, the Simpleton of the North Mountain replied: 'Surely it is you who are narrow-minded and unreasonable. You are not to be compared with the widow's son, despite his puny strength. Though I myself must die, I shall leave a son behind me, and through him a grandson. That grandson will beget sons in his turn, and those soils will also have sons and grandsons. With all this posterity, my line will not die out, while on the other hand the mountain will receive no increment or addition. Why then should I despair of levelling it to the ground at last? The Wise Old Man of the River-bend had nothing to say in reply.

One of the serpent-brandishing deities heard of the undertaking and, fearing that it might never be finished, went and told God Almighty, who was touched by the old man's simple faith, and commanded the two sons of K'ua O to transport the mountains, one to the extreme north-east, the other to the southern comer of Yung.

In the south-west. That is, as far apart as possible. K'ua O was apparently a god of strength.

Ever since then, the region lying between Chi in the north and Han in the south has been ap. unbroken plain.

Roughly, the modem province of Honan.

* * *

Kung-hu of Lu and Ch'i-ying of Chao both fell ill at the same time, and called in the aid of the great Pien-ch'iao.

A famous physician of the fifth century B.C.

Pien-ch'iao cured them both, and when they were well again he told them that the malady they had been suffering from was one that attacked the internal organs from without, and for that reason was curable by the application of vegetable and mineral drugs. 'But,' he added, 'each of you is also the victim of a congenital disease, which has grown along with the body itself. Would you like me now to grapple with this? They said, 'Yes'; but asked to hear his diagnosis first. Pien-ch'iao turned to Kung-hu. 'Your mental powers,' he said, 'are strong, but your willpower is weak. Hence, though fruitful in plans, you are lacking in decision. Ch'i-ying's mental powers, on the other hand, are weak, while his will-power is strong. Hence there is want of forethought, and he is placed at a disadvantage by the narrowness of his aim. Now, if I can effect an exchange of hearts between you, the good will be equally balanced in both.'

That is, Kung-hu, who has the weaker character, will get weaker brain-power to match, while Ch'i-ying, with the stronger will, receives a stronger mind to direct it. Though it may be that Ch'i-ying has the best of the bargain, each man, under the new arrangement, will at any rate be perfectly well balanced. The heart, as we have seen, was regarded as the seat of the mental faculties.

So saying, Pien-ch'iao administered to each of them a potion of medicated wine, which threw them into a death-like trance lasting three days.

A striking proof of the knowledge and practical application of anæsthetics at a very early date.

Then, making an incision in their breasts, he took out each man's heart and placed it in the other's body, poulticing the wounds with herbs of marvellous efficacy.

When the two men regained consciousness, they looked exactly the same as before; and, taking their leave, they returned home. Only it was Kung-hu who went to Ch'i-ying's house, where Ch'i-ying's wife and children naturally did not recognize him, while Ch'i-ying went to Kung-hu's house and was not recognized either. This led to a lawsuit between the two families, and Pien-ch'iao was called in as arbitrator. On his explaining how the matter stood, peace was once more restored.

*   *   *

King Mu of Chou made a tour of inspection in the west. He crossed the K'un-lun range, but turned back before he reached the Yen mountains.

'The place where the sun sets.'

On his return journey, before arriving in China, a certain artificer was presented to him, by name Yen Shih. King Mu received him in audience, and asked what he could do. 'I will do anything,' replied Yen Shih, 'that your Majesty may please to command. But there is a piece of work, already finished, that I should like to submit first to your Majesty's inspection.' 'Bring it with you to-morrow.' said the King, 'and we will look at it together.' So Yen Shih called again the next day, and was duly admitted to the royal presence. 'Who is that man accompanying you?' asked the King. 'That, Sire, is my own handiwork. He can sing and he can act.' The King stared at the figure in astonishment. It walked with rapid strides, moving its head up and down, so that any one would have taken it for a live human being. The artificer touched its chin, and it began singing, perfectly in tune. He touched its hand, and it started posturing, keeping perfect time. It went through any number of movements that fancy might happen to dictate. The King, looking on with his favourite concubine and the other inmates of his harem, could hardly persuade himself that it was not real.

As the performance was drawing to an end, the automaton winked his eye and made sundry advances to the ladies in attendance on the King. This, however, threw the King into a passion, and he would have put Yen Shih to death on the spot had not the latter, in mortal terror, instantly pulled the automaton to pieces to let him see what it really was. And lo! it turned out to be merely a conglomeration of leather, wood, glue and paint, variously coloured white, black, red and blue. Examining it closely, the King found all the internal organs complete--liver, gall, heart, lungs, spleen, kidneys, stomach and intestines--and, over these, again, muscles and bones and limbs with their joints, skin and teeth and hair, all of them artificial. Not a part but was fashioned with the utmost nicety and skill; and when it was put together again, the figure presented the same appearance as when first brought in. The King tried the effect of taking away the heart, and found that the mouth would no longer utter a sound; he took away the liver, and the eyes could no longer see; he took away the kidneys, and the legs lost their power of locomotion.

Now the King was delighted. Drawing a deep breath, he exclaimed: 'Can it be that human skill is really on a par with that of the Creator?' And forthwith he gave an order for two extra chariots, in which he took home with him the artificer and his handiwork.

Now, Pan Shu, with his cloud-scaling ladder, and Mo Ti, with his flying kite, thought that they had reached the limits of human achievement.

'Pan Shu made a cloud-ladder by which he could mount to the sky and assail the heights of heaven; Mo Ti made a wooden kite which would fly for three days without coming down.'

But when Yen Shih's wonderful piece of work had been brought to their knowledge, the two philosophers never again ventured to boast of their mechanical skill, and ceased to busy themselves so frequently with the square and compasses.

*　　*　　*

Hei Luan of Wei had a secret grudge against Ch'iu Ping-chang, for which he slew him; and Lai Tan, the son of Ch'iu Ping-chang, plotted vengeance against his father's enemy. Lai Tan's spirit was very fierce, but his body was very slight. You could count the grains of rice that he ate, and he was at the mercy of every gust of wind. For all the anger in his heart, he was not strong enough to take his revenge in open fight, and he was ashamed to seek help from others. So he swore that, sword in hand, he would cut Hei Luan's throat unawares. This Hei Luan was the most ferocious character of his day, and in brute strength he was a match for a hundred men. His bones and sinews, skin and flesh were cast in superhuman mould. He would stretch out his neck to the blade or bare his breast to the arrow, but the sharp steel would bend or break, and his body show no scar from the Impact. Trusting to his native strength, he looked disdainfully upon Lai Tan as a mere fledgling.

Lai Tan had a friend Shên T'o, who said to him: 'You have a bitter feud against Hei Luan, and Hei Luan treats you with sovereign contempt. What is your plan of action? Shedding tears, Lai Tan besought his friend's counsel. 'Well,' said Shên T'o, 'I am told that K'ung Chou of Wei has inherited, through an ancestor, a sword formerly possessed by the Yin Emperors, of such magical power that a mere boy wielding it can put to flight the embattled hosts of an entire army. Why not sue for the loan of this sword? Acting on this advice, Lai Tan betook himself to Wei and had an interview with K'ung Chou. Following the usage of supplicants, he first went through the ceremony of handing over his wife and children, and then stated his request. 'I have three swords, I replied K'ung Chou, 'but with none of them can you kill a man. You may choose which you like. First, however, let me describe their qualities. The first sword is called "Light-absorber". It is invisible to the eye, and when you swing it you cannot tell that there is anything there. Things struck by it retain an unbroken surface, and it will pass through a man's body without his knowing it. The second is called "Shadow-receiver". If you face north and examine it at the point of dawn, when darkness melts into light, or in the evening, when day gives way to dusk, it appears misty and dim, as though there were something there, the shape of which is not discernible. Things struck by it give out a low sound, and it passes through men's bodies without causing them any pain. The third is called "Night-tempered", because in broad daylight you only see its outline and not the brightness of its blade, while at night you see not the sword itself but the dazzling light which it emits.

'Alluding to its reflecting power.'

The objects which it strikes are cleft through with a sibilant sound, but the line of cleavage closes up immediately. Pain is felt, but no blood remains on the blade.

'These three precious heirlooms have been handed down for thirteen generations, but have never been in actual use. They lie stored away in a box, the seals of which have never been broken.' 'In spite of what you tell me,' said Lai Tan, 'I should like to borrow the third sword.' K'ung Chou then returned his wife and children to him, and they fasted together for seven days. On the seventh day, in the dusk of evening, he knelt down and presented the third sword to Lai Tan, who received it with two low obeisances and went home again.

'He chose the third of the swords because it could be both handled and seen.'

Grasping his new weapon, Lai Tan now sought out his enemy, and found him lying in a drunken stupor at his window. He cut clean through his body in three places between the neck and the navel, but Hei Luan was quite unconscious of it. Thinking he was dead, Lai Tan made off as fast as he could, and happening to meet Hei Luan's son at the door, he struck at him three times with his sword. But it was like hitting the empty air. Hei Luan's son laughed and said: 'Why are you motioning to me in that silly way with your hand?

It will be remembered that the sword was invisible in daylight.

Realizing at last that the sword had no power to kill a man, Lai Tan heaved a sigh and returned home.

When Hei Luan recovered from the effects of his debauch, he was angry With his wife: 'What do you mean by letting me lie exposed to a draught?' he growled; 'it has given me a sore throat and aching pains in the small of my back.' 'Why,' said his son, 'I am also feeling a pain in my body, and a stiffness in my limbs. Lai Tan, you know, was here a little time ago and, meeting me at the door, made three gestures, which seem somehow to have been the cause of it. How he hates us, to be sure!'

Thus, the improper use of divine weapons only leads to discomfiture. in this allegory, Lieh Tzu is satirizing the blood-feud, which must have been a terrible feature of the lawless times in which he lived. The powerlessness of the magic sword to kill may symbolically represent the essential futility of the vendetta which perpetuates itself from father to son.

Book VI - Effort and Destiny

Effort said to Destiny:

I have purposely avoided the familiar modern terms, Fate and Free will, which might seem to furnish the best equivalent to *li* and *ming*. *Li* is the ordinary word for 'strength' or 'force,' and here indicates human effort exerted in some definite direction (the German 'streben') as opposed to the blind and unconscious workings of Nature or Tao.

'Your achievements are not equal to mine.' 'Pray what do you achieve in the working of things,' replied Destiny, 'that you would compare yourself With me? 'Why,' said Effort, 'the length of man's life, his measure of success, his rank, and his wealth, are all things which I have the power to determine.' To this, Destiny made reply: 'P'êng Tsu's wisdom did not exceed that of Yao and Shun, yet he lived to the age of eight hundred. Yen Yüan's ability was not inferior to that of the average man, yet he died at the early age of thirty-two. The virtue of Confucius was not less than that of the feudal princes, yet he was reduced to sore straits between Ch'ên and Ts'ai.

See *The Sayings of Confucius*, p. 115.

The conduct of Chou, of the Yin dynasty, did not surpass that of the Three Men of Virtue, yet he occupied a kingly throne.

Wei Tzu, Chi Tzu and Pi Kan were all relatives of Chou Hsin, by whose orders the last-named was disembowelled.

Chi Cha would not accept the overlordship of Wu, while T'ien Hêng usurped sole power in Ch'i. Po I and Shu. Ch'i starved to death at Shou-yang, while Chi Shih waxed rich at Chan-ch'in. If these results were compassed by your efforts, how is it that you allotted long life to P'êng Tsu and an untimely death to Yen Yüan; that you awarded discomfiture to the sage and success to the impious, humiliation to the wise man and high honours to the fool, poverty to the good and wealth to the wicked? 'If, as you say,' rejoined Effort, 'I have really no control over events, is it not, then, owing to your management that things turn out as they do? Destiny replied: 'The very name "Destiny"

Something already immutably fixed.

shows that there can be no question of management in the case. When the way is straight, I push on; when it is crooked, I put up with it. Old age and early death, failure and success, high rank and humble station, riches and poverty--all these come naturally and of themselves. How can I know anything about them?

'Being what it is, without knowing why--that is the meaning of Destiny. What room is there for management here?

*   *   *

Yang Chu had a friend called Chi Liang, who fell ill. In seven days' time his illness had become very grave; medical aid was summoned, and his sons stood weeping round his bed. Chi Liang said to Yang Chu: 'Such excess of emotion shows my children to be degenerate. Will you kindly sing them something which will enlighten their minds? Yang Chu then chanted the following words:

'How can men be aware of things outside God's ken? Over misfortune man has no control, and can look for no help from God. Have doctors and wizards this knowledge that you and I have not?

The sons, however, did not understand, and finally called in three physicians, Dr Chiao, Dr Yü and Dr Lu. They all diagnosed his complaint; and Dr Chiao delivered his opinion first: 'The hot and cold elements of your body,' he said to Chi Liang, 'are not in harmonious accord, and the impermeable and infundibular parts are mutually disproportionate. The origin of your malady is traceable to disordered appetites, and to the dissipation of your vital essence through worry and care. Neither God nor devil is to blame. Although the illness is grave, it is amenable to treatment.' Chi Liang said: 'You are only one of the common ruck,' and speedily got rid of him. Then Dr Yü came forward and said: 'You were born with too

64

little nervous force, and were too freely fed with mother's milk. Your illness is not one that has developed in a matter of twenty-four hours; the causes which have led up to it are of gradual growth. It is incurable.' Chi Liang replied: 'You are a good doctor,' and told them to give him some food. Lastly, Dr Lu said: 'Your illness is attributable neither to God, nor to man, nor to the agency of spirits. It was already fore-ordained in the mind of Providence when you were endowed with this bodily form at birth. What possible good can herbs and drugs do you? 'You are a heaven-born physician indeed!' cried Chi Liang; and he sent him away laden with presents.

Not long after, his illness disappeared of itself.

*   *   *

Duke Ching of Ch'i was travelling across the northern flank of the Ox-mountain in the direction of the capital. Gazing at the view before him, he burst into a flood of tears, exclaiming: 'What a lovely scene! How verdant and luxuriantly wooded! To think that some day I must die and leave my kingdom, passing away like running water! If only there were no such things as death, nothing should induce me to stir from this spot.' Two of the Ministers in attendance on the Duke, taking their cue from him, also began to weep, saying: 'We, who are dependent on your Highness's bounty, whose food is of an inferior sort, who have to ride on broken-down hacks or in creaking carts--even we do not want to die. How much less our sovereign liege!'

Yen Tzu, meanwhile, was standing by, with a broad smile on his face. The Duke wiped away his tears and, looking at him, said: 'To-day I am stricken with grief on my journey, and both K'ung and Chü mingle their tears with mine. How is it that you alone can smile? Yen Tzu replied: 'If the worthy ruler were to remain in perpetual possession of his realm, Duke T'ai and Duke Huan would still be exercising their sway. If the bold ruler were to remain in perpetual possession, Duke Chuang and Duke Ling would still be ruling the land. But if all these rulers were now in possession, where would your Highness be? Why, standing in the furrowed fields, clad in coir cape and hat!

The ordinary garb of a Chinese peasant in wet weather.

Condemned to a hard life on earth, you would have had no time, I warrant, for brooding over death. Again, how did you yourself come to occupy this throne? By a series of successive reigns and removals, until at last your turn came. And are you alone going to weep and lament over this order of things? That is pure selfishness. it was the sight of these two objects--a self-centred prince and his fawning attendants--that set me quietly laughing to myself just now.'

Duke Ching felt much ashamed. Raising his goblet, he fined himself one cup, and his obsequious courtiers two cups of wine apiece.

*　　*　　*

There was once a man, Tung-mên Wu of Wei, who when his son died testified no grief. His house-steward said to him: 'The love you bore your son could hardly be equalled by that of any other parent. Why, then, do you not mourn for him now that he is dead? 'There was a time,' replied Tung-mên Wu, 'when I had no son, yet I never had occasion to grieve on that account. Now that my son is dead, I am only in the same condition as I was before my son was born. What reason have I, then, to mourn?

There is a story of Plutarch consoling his wife in exactly similar terms after the death of their daughter.

The husbandman takes his measures according to the season, the trader occupies himself with gain, the craftsman strives to master his art, the official pursues power. Here we have the operation of human forces.

But the husbandman has seasons of rain and seasons of drought, the trader meets with gains and losses, the craftsman experiences both failure and success, the official finds opportunities or the reverse. Here we see the working of Destiny.

Book VII - Causality

In the course of Lieh Tzu's instruction by Hu-ch'iu Tzu-lin, the latter said to him: 'You must familiarize yourself with the theory of consequents before you can talk of regulating conduct.' Lieh Tzu said: 'Will you explain what you mean by the theory of consequents?' 'Look at your shadow,' said his Master, 'and then you will know.' Lieh turned and looked at his shadow. When his body was bent, the shadow was crooked; when his body was upright, the shadow was straight. Thus it appeared that the attributes of straightness and crookedness were not inherent in the shadow, but corresponded to certain positions of the body. Likewise, contraction and extension are not inherent in the subject, but take place in obedience to external causes. Holding this theory of consequents is to be at home in the antecedent.

The Law of Causality is the foundation of all science.

Kuan Yin spoke to the Master Lieh Tzu, saying: 'If speech is sweet, the echo will be sweet; if speech is harsh, the echo will be harsh. If the body is long, the shadow will be long; if the body is short, the shadow will be short. Reputation is like an echo, personal experiences like a shadow.

Hence the saying: "Heed your words, and they will meet with harmonious response; heed your actions, and they will find agreeable accord." Therefore, the Sage observes the origin in order to know the issue, scrutinizes the past in order to know the future. Such is the principle whereby he attains foreknowledge.

'The standard of conduct lies with one's own self; the testing of it lies with other men. We are impelled to love those who love us, and to hate those who hate us. T'ang and Wu loved the Empire, and therefore each became King. Chieh and Chou hated the Empire, and therefore they perished. Here we have the test applied. He who does not follow Tao when standard and test are both clear may be likened to one who, when leaving a house, does not go by the door, Or, when travelling abroad, does not keep to the straight road. To seek profit in this way is surely impossible.

'No one has ever profited himself by opposing natural law.'

'You may consider the virtues of Shen Nung and Yu. Yen, you may examine the books of Yü, Hsia, Shang and Chou, you may weigh the utterances of great teachers and sages, but you will find no instance of preservation or destruction, fullness or decay, which has not obeyed this supreme Law.'

Of Causality.

Lieh Tzu learned archery and, when he was able to hit the target, he asked the opinion of Kuan Yin Tzu on his shooting. 'Do you know *why* you hit the target?' said Kuan Yin Tzu. 'No, I do not,' was the reply. 'Then you are not good enough yet,' rejoined Kuan Yin Tzu. Lieh Tzu withdrew and practised for three years after which he again presented himself. Kuan Yin Tzu asked, as before: 'Do you know *why* you hit the target? 'Yes,' said Lieh Tzu, 'I do.' 'In that case, all is well. Hold that knowledge fast, and do not let it slip.'

'Mental and bodily equilibrium are to be sought within oneself. Once you know the causal process which makes you hit the target, you will be able to determine the operation of Destiny beforehand, and when you let fly you will make no mistake.'

The above principle does not apply only to shooting, but also to the government of a State and to personal conduct. Therefore the Sage investigates not the mere facts of preservation and destruction, but rather the causes which bring them about.

* * *

Lieh Tzu said: 'Those who excel in beauty become vain; those who excel in strength become violent. To such, it is useless to speak of Tao. He who is not yet turning grey will surely err if he but speak of Tao; how much less can he put it into practice!

'No man will confide in one who shows himself aggressive. And he in whom no man confides will remain solitary and without support.

'The arrogant and the aggressive will accept no confidences, even if they are made. Their mental attitude to others is one of distrust, and they keep their ears and eyes blocked. Who can render them assistance?'

'The wise man puts his trust in others: thus he reaches fullness of years without decay, perfection of Wisdom without bewilderment. In the government of a State, then, the hardest thing is to recognize the worth of others, not to rely upon one's own.'

'If you succeed in recognizing worth, then the wise will think out plans for you, and the able will act for you. By never rejecting talent from outside, you will find the State easy to govern.'

*   *   *

There was once a man in Sung who carved a mulberry leaf out of jade for his prince. It took three years to complete, and it mutated Nature so exquisitely in its down, its glossiness, and its general configuration from tip to stem, that, if placed in a heap of real mulberry leaves, it could not be distinguished from them. This man was subsequently pensioned by the Sung State as a reward for his skill. Lieh Tzu, hearing of it, said: 'If it took the Creator three years to make a single leaf, there would be very few trees with leaves on them. The Sage will rely not so much on human science and skill as on the operations of Tao.'

*   *   *

The Master Lieh Tzu was very poor, and his face wore a hungry look. A certain stranger spoke about it to Tzu Yang, of Cheng. 'Lieh Yü-k'ou,' said he, 'is a scholar in possession of Tao. Yet here he is, living in destitution, within your Excellency's dominion. It surely cannot be that you have no liking for scholars? Tzu Yang forthwith directed that an official allowance of grain should be sent to him. Lieh Tzu came out to receive the messengers, made two low bows and declined the gift, whereupon the messengers went away, and

Lieh Tzu reentered the house. There he was confronted by his Wife, who beat her breast and cried aloud: 'I have always understood that the wife and family of a man of Tao live a fife of ease and pleasure. Yet now, when his Honour sends you a present of food, on account of your starved appearance, you refuse to accept it! I suppose you will call that "destiny"!' The Master Lieh Tzu smiled and replied: 'The Minister did not know about me himself. His present of grain was made on the suggestion of another. If it had been a question of punishing me, that too would have been done at some one else's prompting. That is the reason why I did not accept the gift.'

Later on, the masses rose in actual rebellion against Tzu Yang, and slew him.

It is implied that Lieh Tzu's independence of spirit saved his life, inasmuch as a pensioner would have shared the fate of his patron.

*   *   *

Mr Shih of Lu had two sons, one of whom was a scholar and the other a soldier. The former found in his accomplishments the means of ingratiating himself with the Marquis of Ch'i, who engaged him as tutor to the young princes. The other brother proceeded to Ch'u, and won favour with the King of that State by his military talents. The King was so well pleased that he installed him at the head of his troops. Thus both of them succeeded in enriching their family and shedding lustre on their kinsfolk.

Now, a certain Mr Mêng, the neighbour of Mr Shih, also had two sons who followed the selfsame professions but were straitened by poverty. Envying the affluence of the Shih family, Mr Mêng called at his neighbour's house, and wanted to know the secret of their rapid rise in the world. The two brothers readily gave him the desired information, whereupon the eldest son immediately set off for Ch'in, hoping that his cultural attainments would recommend him to the King of that State. But the King said: 'At the present moment all the feudal princes are struggling to outbid one another in power, and the great essential is to keep up a large army. If I tried to govern my State on the lines of benevolence and righteousness, ruin and annihilation would be the outcome! So saying, he had the unfortunate man castrated, and turned him away.

The second son, meanwhile, had gone to Wei, hoping that his military knowledge would stand him in good stead. But the Marquis of Wei said to himself--'Mine is a weak State hedged in by powerful ones.

Wei was bounded by Chin and Ch'i on the north, Lu on the east, and Chêng on the south.

My method of preserving tranquillity is to show subservience to the larger States and to conciliate the lesser ones. If I were to rely on armed force, I could only expect utter destruction. I must not allow this man to depart unscathed, or he may find his way to some other State and be a terrible thorn in my side.' So, without more ado, he cut off his feet and sent him back to Lu.

On their return, the whole family fell to beating their breasts in despair, and uttered imprecations on Mr Shih. Mr Shih, however, said: 'Success consists in hitting off the right moment, while missing it means failure. Your method was identical with ours, only the result was different. That is not due to any flaw in the action itself, but simply because it was not well timed. Nothing, in the ordering of this world, is either at all times right or at all times wrong. What formerly passed current may nowadays be rejected; what is now rejected may by and by come into use again. The fact that a thing is in use or in disuse forms no criterion whatever of right or wrong. There is no fixed rule for seizing opportunities, hitting off the right moment, or adapting oneself to circumstances; it is all a matter of native wit. If you are deficient in that, you may possess the learning of a Confucius or the strategical gifts of a Lü Shang, and yet you will remain poor wherever you go.

The Mêng family were now 'in a more resigned frame of mind, and their indignation had subsided. 'Yes, you are right,' they said; 'please say no more about it.'

*   *   *

Duke Wên of Chin put an army into the field with the intention of attacking the Duke of Wei, whereat Tzu Ch'u threw his head back and laughed aloud. On being asked the reason of his behaviour, he replied: 'I was thinking of the experience of a neighbour of mine, who was escorting his wife on a visit to her own family. On the way, he came across a woman tending silkworms, who attracted him greatly, and he fell into conversation with her. Happening to look up, what should he see but his own wife also receiving the attentions of an admirer! It was the recollection of this incident that made me laugh.'

The Duke saw the point, and forthwith turned home with his army. Before he got back, an invading force had already crossed his northern frontier!

'As you behave to others, so others will behave to you. He who rides roughshod towards the accomplishment of his own desires, in the belief that it will not occur to others to do the like, will in all probability find himself circumstanced as above.'

*   *   *

In the Chin State, which was infested with robbers, there lived a certain Ch'i Yung, who was able to tell a robber by his face; by examining the expression of his eyes he could read his inmost thoughts. The Marquis of Chin employed him in the inspection of hundreds and thousands of robbers, and he never missed a single one. The Marquis expressed his delight to Wên Tzu of Chao, saying: 'I have a man who, singlehanded, is ridding my whole State of robbers. He saves me the necessity of employing a whole staff of police.' Wên Tzu replied: 'If your Highness relies on a detective for catching robbers, you will never get rid of them. And what is more, Ch'i Yung is certain sooner or later to meet with a violent end.'

Meanwhile, a band of robbers were plotting together. 'Ch'i Yung,' they said, 'is the enemy who is trying to exterminate us.' So one day they stole upon him in a body and murdered him. When the Marquis of Chin heard the news, he was greatly alarmed and immediately sent for Wên Tzu. 'Your prophecy has come true,' he said;

72

'Ch'i Yung is dead. What means can I adopt for catching robbers now? 'in Chou,' replied Wên Tzu, 'we have a proverb: "Search not the ocean-depths for fish: calamity comes upon those who pry into hidden mysteries." If you want to be quit of robbers, the best thing your Highness can do is to promote the worthy to office. Let them instruct and enlighten their sovereign on the one hand, and reform the masses below them on the other. if once the people acquire a sense of shame, you will not find them turning into robbers.'

The Marquis then appointed Sui Hui to be Prime Minister, and all the robbers fled to the Ch'in State.

A shrewd thrust at the brigand State which eventually swallowed up all the rest. The commentator says: 'Apply cleverness to ferret out wrongdoing, and the cunning rogue will escape. Using the gift of intuition to expose crime only excites hatred in the wicked. That "sagacity is an evil" is no empty saying.'

* * *

Duke Mu of Ch'in said to Po Lo:

A famous judge of horses, of whom Chuang Tzu speaks with scant respect. See *Musings of a Chinese Mystic*, p. 66.

'You are now advanced in years. Is there any member of your family whom I could employ to look for horses in your stead?' Po Lo replied: 'A good horse can be picked out by its general build and appearance. But the superlative horse--one that raises no dust and leaves no tracks--is something evanescent and fleeting, elusive as thin air. The talent of my sons lies on a lower plane altogether: they can tell a good horse when they see one, but they cannot tell a superlative horse. I have a friend, however, one Chiu-fang Kao, a hawker of fuel and vegetables, who in things appertaining to horses is nowise my inferior. Pray see him.'

Duke Mu did so, and subsequently despatched him on the quest for a steed. Three months later, he returned with the news that he had found one. 'It is now in Sha-ch'iu,' he added. 'What kind of a horse is it?' asked the Duke. 'Oh, it is a dun-coloured mare,' was the reply. However, on some one being sent to fetch it, the animal turned out to be a coal-black stallion! Much displeased, the Duke sent for Po Lo. 'That friend of yours,' he said, 'whom I commissioned to look for a horse, has made a nice mess of it. Why, he cannot even distinguish a beast's colour or sex! What on earth can he know about horses?' Po Lo heaved a sigh of satisfaction. 'Has he really got as far as that?' he cried. 'Ah, then he is worth a thousand of me put together. There is no comparison between us. What Kao keeps in view is the spiritual mechanism. In making sure of the essential, he forgets the homely details; intent on the inward qualities, he loses sight of the external. He sees what he wants to see, and not what he does not want to see. He looks at the things he ought to look at, and neglects those that need not be looked at. So clever a judge of horses is Kao, that he has it in him to judge something better than horses.'

When the horse arrived, it turned out indeed to be a superlative horse.

*　　*　　*

Mr Yü was a wealthy man of the Liang State.

Another name for the Wei State in the fourth century B.C.

His household was rolling in riches, and his hoards of money and silk and other valuables were quite incalculable. It was his custom to have banquets served, to the accompaniment of music, in a high upper hall overlooking the main road; there he and his friends would sit drinking their wine and amusing themselves with bouts of gambling.

One day, a party of young gallants happened to pass along the road. In the chamber above, play was going on as usual, and a lucky throw of the dice, which resulted in the capture of both fishes, evoked a loud burst of merriment from the players.

The game here alluded to was played on a board with a 'river' in the middle.

Precisely at that moment, it happened that a kite which was sailing overhead dropped the carcass of a rat in the midst of the company outside. The young men held an angry consultation on the spot: 'This Mr Yü,' they said, 'has been enjoying his wealth for many a long day, and has always treated his neighbours in the most arrogant spirit. And now, although we have never offended him, he insults us with this dead art. If such an outrage goes unavenged, the world will look upon us as a set of poltroons. Let us summon up our utmost resolution, and combine with one accord to wipe him and his family out of existence!' The whole party signified their agreement, and when the evening of the day appointed had come, they collected, fully armed for the attack, and exterminated every member of the family.

'Pride and extravagance lead to calamity and ruin in more ways than one. Mr. Yü's family was destroyed, although in this particular instance he had no thought of insulting others; nevertheless, the catastrophe was due to an habitual lack of modesty and courtesy in his conduct.'

*   *   *

In the east of China there was a man named Yüan Ching Mu, who set off on a journey but was overcome by hunger on the way. A certain robber from Hu-fu, of the name of Ch'iu, saw him lying there, and fetched a bowl of rice-gruel in order to feed him. After swallowing three mouthfuls, Yüan Ching Mu opened his eyes and murmured, 'Who are you?' 'I am a native of Hu-fu, and my name is Ch'iu.' 'Oh misery!' cried Yüan Ching Mu, 'are not you the robber Ch'iu? What are you feeding me for? I am an honest man and cannot eat your food.' So saying, he clutched the ground with both hands, and began retching and coughing in order to bring it up again. Not succeeding, however, he fell flat on his face and expired.

Now the man from Hu-fu was a robber, no doubt, but the food he brought was not affected thereby. Because a man is a robber, to refuse to eat the food he offers you, on the ground that it is tainted with crime, is to have lost all power of discriminating between the normal and the real.

*   *   *

Yang Chu's younger brother, named Pu, went out one day wearing a suit of white clothes. It came on to ram, so that he had to change and came back dressed in a suit of black. His dog failed to recognize him in this garb, and rushed out at him, barking. This made Yang Pu angry, and he was going to give the dog a beating, when Yang Chu said: 'Do not beat him. You are no wiser than he. For, suppose your dog went away white and came home black, do you mean to tell me that you would not think it strange?

*   *   *

Yang Chu said:, You may do good without thinking about fame, but fame will follow in its wake. Fame makes no tryst with gain, but gain will come all the same. Gain makes no tryst with strife, but strife will certainly ensue. Therefore the superior man is very cautious about doing good.'

*   *   *

The good people of Han-tan were in the habit, every New Year's day, of presenting their Governor, Chien Tzu, with a number of live pigeons. This pleased the Governor very much, and he liberally rewarded the donors. To a stranger who asked the meaning of the custom, Chien Tzu explained that the release of living creatures on New Year's day was the sign of a benevolent disposition. 'But,' rejoined the stranger, 'the people, being aware of your Excellency's whim, no doubt exert themselves to catch as many pigeons as possible, and large numbers must get killed in the process. If you really wish to let the birds live, the best way would be to prohibit the people from capturing them at all. If they have to be caught first in order to be released, the kindness does not compensate for the cruelty.' Chien Tzu acknowledged that he was right.

*   *   *

Mr T'ien, of the Ch'i State, was holding an ancestral banquet in his hall, to which a thousand guests were bidden. As he sat in their midst, many came up to him with presents of fish and game. Eyeing them approvingly, he exclaimed with unction: 'How generous is Almighty God to man! He makes the five kinds of grain to grow, and

creates the finny and the feathered tribes, especially for our benefit.' All Mr T'ien's guests applauded this sentiment to the echo; but
the twelve-year-old son of a Mr Pao, regardless of seniority, came
forward and said: 'You are wrong, my lord. All the living creatures
of the universe stand in the same category as ourselves, and one is
of no greater intrinsic value than another. It is only by reason of
size, strength or cunning that some particular species gains the
mastery, or that one preys upon another. None of them are produced in order to subserve the uses of others. Man catches and eats
those that are fit for food, but how can it be maintained that God
creates these expressly for man's use? Mosquitoes and gnats suck
man's blood, and tigers and wolves devour his flesh; but we do not
therefore assert that God created man expressly for the benefit of
mosquitoes and gnats, or to provide food for tigers and wolves.'

In reading these words, penned before the beginning of our era,
it is curious to reflect that only about fifty years ago Christian tele-
ology used solemnly to preach this very doctrine of 'design', until
Darwin arose and swept it away for ever.

*　　*　　*

A man, having lost his axe, suspected his neighbour's son of having taken it. Certain peculiarities in his gait, his countenance and
his speech, marked him out as the thief. In his actions, his movements, and in fact his whole demeanour, it was plainly written that
he and no other had stolen the axe. By and by, however, while dig-
ging in a dell, the owner came across the missing implement. The
next day, when he saw his neighbour's son again, he found no trace
of guilt in his movements, his actions, or his general demeanour.

'The man in whose mind suspicion is at work will let himself be
carried away by utterly distorted fancies, until at last he sees white
as black, and detects squareness in a circle.'

*　　*　　*

There was once a man in the Ch'i State who had a burning lust for
gold. Rising early one morning, he dressed and put on his hat and

went down to the marketplace, where he proceeded to seize and carry off the gold from a money-changer's shop.

An ordinary thief would have gone at night, and probably naked, after smearing his body with oil.

He was arrested by the police, who were puzzled to know why he had committed the theft at a time when every body was about. 'When I was taking the gold,' he replied, 'I did not see anybody at all; what I saw was the gold, and nothing but the gold.'